D0876611

EX AFRICA:

The Ten Stages of My Life From the Niger Delta to Nashville, Tennessee

Mebenin Awipi

authorHOUSE®

AuthorHouse™
1663 Liberty Drive
Bloomington, IN 47403
www.authorhouse.com
Phone: 1-800-839-8640

© 2011 Mebenin Awipi. All rights reserved.

No part of this book may be reproduced, stored in
a retrieval system, or transmitted by any means
without the written permission of the author.

First published by AuthorHouse 5/18/2011

ISBN: 978-1-4567-4986-6 (e)
ISBN: 978-1-4567-4985-9 (sc)

Library of Congress Control Number: 2011904653

Printed in the United States of America

Any people depicted in stock imagery provided
by Thinkstock are models, and such images are
being used for illustrative purposes only.
Certain stock imagery © Thinkstock.

This book is printed on acid-free paper.

Because of the dynamic nature of the Internet, any web
addresses or links contained in this book may have changed
since publication and may no longer be valid. The views
expressed in this work are solely those of the author and do
not necessarily reflect the views of the publisher, and the
publisher hereby disclaims any responsibility for them.

Table of Contents

DEDICATION

TO MY CHILDREN AND THE CHILDREN OF MY EXTENDED
FAMILIES, THE AWIPI AND FARO CLANS IN ISAMPOU, THE
WANZU CLAN IN ANGIAMA AND THE OGIRIGI CLAN IN
OTUAN, ALL IN BAYELSA STATE, NIGERIA.

PREFACE

There are usually some good reasons for writing a book of memories about one's life, and some bad ones. One bad reason is that the writer thinks his life is so important that people would be interested in reading about him. I assure everyone that this is not why I am writing this book. The main reason I am writing this is to share with my children aspects of my life that they did not know, having grown up in circumstances so different from mine, and because the events occurred before they were born or after they had left home to live their own adult lives, or they were too young to fully understand the meaning of events as they happened. The sharing is voluntary and they are not forced or required to read it. In fact, they may not even like all of it, particularly those chapters with reverse anthropology content. But I hope they will not be embarrassed by any part of it. Nevertheless, the book is dedicated to them and their clans of cousins.

Another reason that has motivated me to embark on this project has to do with my ethnic group in Nigeria, one of hundreds that the British colonists refer to as tribes. The Izon people (called Ijaws by colonial officials) live in the riverine areas of the Niger Delta, all along the coast from the Cameroon border on the east to the Benin Republic border on the West, intermingling with some other groups at the borders of their territory. They built their villages on lands that lie between various creeks and branches of the Niger River as it splits into dozens of channels before emptying into the Atlantic Ocean. In some cases, the land is just a strip of island in the swamps with very unstable structural foundation. From lack of archaeological evidence of their origins and surmising from their language and mythological tales, it appears that they migrated from distant lands, perhaps from as far as ancient upper Nile valley and the Sudan, with a stop of significant duration in the old Benin Kingdom, before settling in their present location. The fact that they appear to have adapted so naturally to the creeks and swamps of the Niger Delta suggests an origin from a similar riverine environment. Again, looking at the map of Africa, one observes that besides the River Niger, two other long rivers are the Nile and Congo Rivers, suggesting previous residence in one of those river valleys. Unfortunately, they did not leave behind any written record of their travels and we do not know which of the many causes of forced or voluntary mass migration, such as wars, famine, political or religious persecution, applied to their case. We have lost what might have been an inspiring exodus story. We and all future generations are poorer for it. I therefore urge all Izons wherever they are to leave written records behind for future generations, and I am trying to follow my own advice.

Just to make sure that I do not take myself too seriously, I have decided not to follow conventional biographical sketches by reversing the timeline of my story, going from the present to the past .I have always enjoyed flouting conventional wisdom and some old habits are hard to break. Of course, my remembrance of recent events is more accurate than that of events of forty or fifty years ago, so you are cautioned to take those distant memories with a grain of salt. Still, I hope that any casual reader will find this book interesting, enjoyable, and perhaps, even informative.

I have taken part of my title from the maxim of the Roman naturalist Pliny the Elder, " EX AFRICA SEMPER ALIQUID NOVI ", the English translation being " There is always something new out of Africa ". Pliny was talking of strange plants and animals in his day, but in our day, we hope we can include persons and ideas, knowledge and wisdom. Besides, I try to make some use of my high school Latin studies whenever possible.

Metaphorically, every life is a journey, with a number of turns and stops. This is true even for those who live their lives in one city from cradle to grave. But for one who started life in the Niger Delta, and whose journey has covered tens of thousands of miles, with stops in Princeton University in New Jersey, Columbia University in New York City, Bell Telephone Laboratories in Holmdel, New Jersey and Naperville, Illinois, to Nashville, Tennessee, it has been, literally and symbolically, a long journey.

Over such a long journey, one has, inevitably, made a number of observations and learned a number of lessons. I have found some of these lessons useful in my own life. Perhaps it will be a waste to take all of them with me to my grave. By sharing, they could be useful to another generation of travelers. Welcome aboard.

The various stops of my journey such as those mentioned above roughly form the outline of the book. Chapter One covers the experiences of public service, especially the four years from 2002 to 2006 as a member of the Board of Public Education of Metropolitan Nashville and Davidson County, after benefiting from a " deus ex machina ", also seen as a fortuitous second chance, in the election process. This is followed by chapters on twenty years of teaching at Tennessee State University, Nashville; then there were four years of teaching and administration at the University of Lagos and the Rivers State University of Science and Technology, Port Harcourt, in Nigeria; there were twelve years as a member of the technical staff at Bell Laboratories in Holmdel, New Jersey and Naperville, Illinois. The years of higher education included four years at Columbia University, New York, NY and three years at Princeton University in New Jersey. The years of secondary and primary education were in Government College, Ughelli, Native Administration School, Bomadi and CMS School, Isampou, all in the Niger Delta.

Finally in Chapter Ten, Assessment, I have personally tried to define the purpose of my life, part of the purpose of all human life on earth. Our scientific knowledge has so far been unable to answer this question, as well as any possible life after death. To fill this vacuum, religions have stepped in to provide a variety of answers over many ages and cultures, and we have been required to believe them, no questions asked. Our present day answers may be improvements over those of the Egyptians, Greeks, Romans and countless other cultures on all continents on earth, but we have not spoken the last word on these matters, and in my view, the jury is still out. As intelligent as we human beings are, we have sometimes been too smart for our good, such that when we have no knowledge, we have substituted our imagination in constructing our beliefs. In the process, so many have failed to distinguish between what we know and what we believe. The fear of the unknown has been a useful survival instinct in our biological evolution, but we risk going wrong or doing wrong to others when we fail to know that we do not know. Our best outlook is to keep an open mind and be modest in exercising the power of ignorance, so that whenever some new piece of knowledge contradicts our beliefs, we are not so quick to feel threatened by it and are not easily led into religious wars because of differences in our beliefs.

1: OATH OF OFFICE, 2003

CHAPTER ONE

Public Service: 2002 - 2006

It is hard to say when this crazy idea of running for and serving as an elected public officer took form, and it is a bigger wonder that I actually got to serve for four years. Looking back, I can just trace the outline of a series of brief contacts with the electoral process. First, between 1989 and 1992, as part of the requirement for public and professional service in the university tenure and promotion process, I served as program director, vice-chairman and chairman of the Nashville Section of the Institute of Electrical and Electronics Engineers [IEEE]. The Nashville Section had about four hundred certified members out of over one million IEEE members world-wide; our local elections were usually single candidate contests for each of four officer positions and the number of ballots actually cast ranged from thirty to forty each year. Even though our duties were relatively light, it was still quite exhausting on top of the professional workload of teaching and research as a faculty member that I was quite burnt out for several years when my final year of office ended.

In 1996, a member of my church, Ms. Johniene Thomas, ran for a seat on the school board in the district surrounding our church in the predominantly African-American North Nashville. Even though I did not live in the district, I volunteered to canvass for votes door to door, and experienced the joy of winning one vote at a time, and the agony of rejection and hostility towards the candidate. She ended up losing the contest in a close election with very light turnout; afterwards, she said she could have won had she received a thousand votes.

In 1998, another member of my church, Justice A.A. Birch ran for retention on the Tennessee State Supreme Court after a few years of service on an interim appointment. There was a lot of opposition to candidates that were considered soft on death penalty cases. I volunteered to distribute several hundred flyers in the parking lots of a Kroger's supermarket and shopping mall. He won the statewide contest and served on the court for over ten years, including three years as Chief Justice of the state.

Finally, in 2000, after Vice-President Al Gore moved his Presidential campaign headquarters from Washington, D.C. to Nashville, my son Embeleakpo and I volunteered to work for his election. I was assigned to call registered voters in states with 'N' as first alphabet: Nebraska, New Jersey, New York, North Dakota and North Carolina. We were given a script with talking points as we solicited for support and contributions.

When my daughter Tarimotimi was at the Arts Magnet High School during its incubation at Pearl-Cohn Comprehensive High School, she played the clarinet and then joined the flag corps of the marching band. I became an active member of the Band Boosters of parents and guardians, serving the students with refreshments during performances at football games and in parades on other occasions. In my daughter's junior year, 1995, I was nominated to serve as President of the PCHS Band Boosters, but my teaching schedule that fall semester included a laboratory section from 5 to 7 PM on Fridays. Since many of our band booster meetings and services took place on Friday nights before, during and after football games at home and throughout the mid-state, I thought I could not serve satisfactorily if I could not be physically present at those critical occasions, and therefore declined the nomination.

After my daughter's graduation from high school, and since she was the last child in the family, there was more time for volunteer activities. In the senior year, she received many awards and honors, and we were summoned to school board meetings to be recognized. We were there for successive stages of the National Merit scholarship competition and for graduation as valedictorian of her class. On several of those occasions, I picked up the agenda package and stayed for some time to observe the discussions and activities of the board, and finally concluded that this was something I could do well that could also be a contribution to the community in return for the benefits of education that my children had received.

So in 2000, I started to inquire into the process of being elected to serve on the Board of Public Education of Metropolitan Nashville and Davidson County. First, I could only run in a district that includes my place of residence. There are nine seats on the board and so the county is divided into nine districts with approximately equal populations. After the 2000 census, all the district boundaries were redrawn by the planning department; at first, my district was labeled District 2, but this was corrected in the final designation as District 6. Second, the section of the Metro Nashville Charter Law which established the board also specifies two alternating cycles for electing members. In 2000, odd-numbered districts would have elections and in 2002, even-numbered districts would have elections. There were no term limits, so members could run and if re-elected, could serve for as long as they wished. So I had to wait until 2002 for a chance to contest in District 6 and I also had to wait to find out if I would be contesting against a popular long term incumbent.

I spent 2001 and early 2002 doing some homework on the duties and responsibilities of the board. I attended several critical board meetings, including the meeting on the appointment of Dr. Pedro Garcia as the Director of Schools. I attended the meetings called by the Planning Department and the Election Commission to explain the boundaries of various election districts and the requirements for getting on the ballot. I also searched among my friends for persons who could serve as my campaign manager and treasurer. I first approached Ms. Thomas about the manager role, but she had committed to another friend who was running for the U.S. House of Representatives. I then approached a former member of my church who had the advantage of living in my district. Mrs. Yvonne Burrows Sawyer and her family were active members of Saint Anselm's Episcopal Church long before my family joined in 1989. Her family left our church in 1999 during a dispute about calling a woman as our priest, but we had continued to keep in touch as friends over the years largely by attendance at weddings, funerals and other rites of passage. When I talked to her about my election ambition early in 2002, she told me that she had also run successfully for a seat on the city council in Lancaster, Pennsylvania before they moved to Nashville and that she would be glad to help me achieve my goal. After settling on a campaign manager, I next persuaded an accountant and owner of a financial management company, Mr. Charles Bright, to serve as my campaign treasurer. He had migrated from Liberia as a victim of political and civil upheaval in that country and was a member of Saint Phillip's Episcopal Church in Donelson, a suburban community of Nashville-Davidson County, where I and two other members of my small congregation also received training as Stephen ministers, laypersons who try to provide comfort to others in grief; we also met frequently at events and conventions of the Episcopal Diocese of Tennessee.

The next step was to pick up nominating petition forms from the Davidson County Election Commission which was the official manner of declaring my intention to run for election and to request that my name be placed on the ballot after verification of my qualifications for the particular office. These qualifications were citizenship and residence in the district, minimum high school diploma, and the names, addresses and signatures of twenty-five registered voters also resident in the district. Yvonne and I took several weeks to collect over forty signatures just to make sure that at least twenty-five were valid registered voters; I showed my certificate of naturalization and my Bachelor's, Master's and doctoral degree diplomas from Princeton and Columbia Universities, to meet the qualification requirements. Of course, showing all those degrees was quite an overkill, but I did not want to show any documents from Nigeria, as I knew that my first generation immigrant status would be an issue in the campaign. Yvonne accompanied me to submit all the documents to the commission, and as soon as this was done, we also sat down for a short interview with Ms. Nichole Troutman, then a reporter for The City Paper, one of Nashville's daily newspapers. Before this, I had viewed the whole process as a lark, with very low expectation of a successful outcome. However, when I saw my name in the headline of the story the next morning, it began to sink in that this was a fairly serious matter. The only previous occasion that I can recall that my name had been in the city's newspapers was when my wife Georgina and I were listed as parents of our daughter in the special "Best and Brightest" report on all high school valedictorians and salutatorians in 1997. One of the most significant duties of the school board was to pass annual budgets for current operations and capital needs of the school district. The operating budget was usually about one third of the entire city budget, and the budget for renovations and construction of schools was about one quarter of the city's capital budget. Thus the management and oversight of these funds were serious public responsibilities.

Immediately after I submitted my papers, the first of a number of strange events took place. I asked the staff person at the election Commission who else had declared an intention to run for the same office. She told me that a lady named Lorinda Hale had done so. This was a surprise to me since I expected to see the name of the incumbent, Mr. Vern Denney, who had held the seat since July 1983. It turned out that Mr. Denney had decided not to seek re-election and had hand-picked Lorinda to take his place. My appearance in the picture was thus a surprise and an annoyance to Lorinda who viewed me as a stranger coming out of nowhere. Needless to say, in the six years that we have known each other, Lorinda and I have said hello to each other no more than twice, first when we both appeared before a Metro Council Committee, and later when we participated in an election debate organized by the League of Women Voters. When it was announced by the Nashville School System that Lorinda's mother passed away in 2004, I sent her a sympathy card, but there was no acknowledgement from her. On my part, I was a little glad that I was not going against a twenty-year incumbent, which could only be an advantage, no matter how slight it turned out to be. To her, I was a nuisance and a fly on the ointment of what had been a done deal and now they had to go through the trouble of finding out who and what I was, with such a strange name and all.

Then the next surprise happened. Mr. Denney had served for over twenty years with little or no compensation and when a vacancy for the position of Director of Student Assignment Services occurred, he decided to take up the appointment as a partial reward for all the years of dedicated service to the school district. Therefore, he resigned his seat on the board of education, since by law he could not serve on the board and be an employee of the district at the same time. This took place in April 2002, four months before the end of his term in August. By law, it was then up to the City Council to appoint an interim member to serve until the election in August.

So we had to write letters to the Council, declaring our

desire to receive the interim appointment and attached our resumes. On the day that the appointment was to be voted on, April 16, 2002, we both appeared before the Council Rules, Confirmations and Public Elections Committee and we both made brief statements before the full Council just before the vote. I was nominated by Howard Gentry, who was then a Council member-at-Large, and argued that if the Council thought that achievement was important in our schools, then they should vote for me, since my resume was six pages long, with degrees from two Ivy League universities, and a host of publications and two United States patents to my credit, granted during my years of employment at Bell Telephone Laboratories, Holmdel, New Jersey in the nineteen seventies. On the other hand, my opponent had a half-page resume, showing she was born in New York state and had graduated from high school in the state of Georgia. During my service as Professor of Electrical Engineering at Tennessee State University, I had got to know Howard as he held several positions in the Athletic Department, the TSU Foundation and the University Development Office; further, his eldest daughter, Christiana, was a cheerleader with the PCHS marching band in the same years as my daughter, so we had been fellow members of the Band Boosters. Especially in lobbying on my behalf behind the scene, he challenged them to declare whether they were going to acknowledge my educational and professional achievements or to show that they would accept someone less as long as it was one of them. As he related the story to two audiences of Nigerian-Americans at fund raising events during his two campaigns for Vice Mayor and for Mayor in 2002 and 2007, he challenged his colleagues aggressively to choose between merit versus being " one of us". Some members bought into his argument, others were willing to vote for me as a symbolic gesture, since the appointment was for only four months, and they had heard that I had very slim chances of prevailing in the general election for a four-year term; they were correct about my chances.

The following are the two paragraphs from the minutes of the Council meeting on April 16, 2002:

"Board of Public Education

The President called for an election to fill the School District 2 vacancy on the Metropolitan Board of Public Education for a term expiring August 31, 2002. Candidates for the position were Ms. Lorinda Hall and Dr. Mebenin Awipi. Ms. Williams, Chair of the Rules-Confirmations-Public Elections Committee, reported that the Committee had interviewed the candidates and declared both to be qualified for the position.

The vote was taken and recorded as follows: Awipi: Ferrell, Gentry, Tucker, Gilmore, Black, Nollner, Hall, Beehan, Campbell, Hart, Balthrop, Greer, Wallace, Haddox, Whitmore, Hand, Holloway, Knoch, Jenkins, Turner, Williams(21): Hall: Waters, Briley, Dillard, Brown, Ponder, Stanley, Loring, McClendon, Hausser, Bogen, Summers, Shulman, Arriola, Sontany, Alexander, Kerstetter, Lineweaver(17). "Abstaining" Majors(1). The President declared that Dr. Awipi was elected to fill the vacancy on the Metropolitan Board of Public Education."

A few items need some explanation; the confusion about the district label, 6 in place of 2, occurred with the redistricting after the 2000 census as previously mentioned. Lorinda's last name is Hale, not Hall, a correction that she churlishly made in the brief statement before the vote; I am sure chastising the council did not win any friends for her, but then she did not think winning friends was necessary as her appointment was supposed to have been a done deal. The Council had forty voting members, made up of 35 district members and 5 at-large members elected by the whole county. Even though one member was absent on that evening, the 21 votes were a minimum majority of the entire council. Ten of the eleven African-Americans on the council voted for me, and one abstained.

I have always considered those twenty-one persons the kind of righteous souls that could have saved the twin cities of Sodom and Gomorrah from destruction as described in Genesis 18. Of course, if God were to send angels to Nashville today, they will find not only twenty-one righteous souls, but twenty-one thousand and more in our city: we are truly blessed. It also reminds me of the words of my church's liturgical reading on All Saints' Day from the book variously known as Wisdom, Ecclesiasticus or Sirach 44: "HYMN IN HONOR OF OUR ANCESTORS", Verse 10: " But these also were godly men [and women], whose righteous deeds have not been forgotten". At the time, I did not know most of them, so I have made an effort to know them better. Some of the information below was obtained from "The 2001 Metro Blue Book, a Citizen's Guide to Metropolitan Government of Nashville and Davidson", published by the Nashville branch of The League of Women Voters:

Chris Ferrell, Member-at- large, graduate of Furman University and Vanderbilt Divinity School; lost to Howard

Gentry in contest for Vice-Mayor in August 2002, later fell into disfavor with the conservative establishment for support a gay rights ordinance, and dropped out of politics;

Howard Gentry, B.S., M.S. Tennessee State University, first African-American Vice-Mayor of Nashville elected in August 2002, and ran a close race for Mayor in 2007;

Dr. Carolyn Baldwin Tucker, African-American retired exemplary educator, earned Bachelor's and Master's degrees from Tennessee State University and Ph.D. from Peabody-Vanderbilt; served two terms as an at-large member of Metro Council;

Mrs. Brenda Harris Gilmore, B.S., M.S. Business and Human Resource Development, Tennessee State University; an African-American lady who was Director of University Mail Service at Vanderbilt; after serving two terms as a district council member, she was elected in 2006 as a Representative to the State of Tennessee General Assembly;

Melvin Black, B.S., Master of Education, Tennessee State University, an African-American retired educator;

Ron Nollner, a native Nashvillian, business owner and Southern Baptist;

Lawrence Hall, Jr., African American graduate of Trevecca Nazarene University in business administration with additional training as a paralegal studies, working for the Tennessee State Legislature;

Eileen Beehan, B.A. in education from Saint Mary's College, Notre Dame, Indiana; Department Director of Catholic Social Services at Catholic Charities of Tennessee;

Earl Campbell, retired fire captain and building superintendent at Madison Church of Christ;

Lawrence Hart, an attorney, B.A. and J.D., University of Tennessee; U.S. Army Command Staff College, Korean Expeditionary Medal;

Mrs. Bettye Balthrop, U.T. Nashville two years- Business; retired kindly grandmother, Presbyterian, lost her bid for reelection for a second term in August 2002;

Ronnie Greer, a young African-American business and family man;

Ludye Wallace, B.S. Political Science, Tennessee State University who had served on the council beyond the term limit of eight years by running to represent a different district;

Morris Haddox, B.S. in Pharmacy, Texas Southern University, an African-American community activist who operated a drugstore on Charlotte Avenue downtown, still being run by his sons;

Edward Whitmore, B.S. Tennessee State University, an African-American concerned about the quality of predominantly black schools in the district;

Norma Hand, retired from Metro Fire Department as an accountant;

Mrs. Saletta Holloway, B.A. in Human Resource Management, Trevecca Nazarene College, who was my council district 29 representative and lobbied diligently for votes on my behalf; her son Walter later majored in electrical engineering at Tennessee State University and took several courses with me;

Don Knoch, B.S. Criminal Justice at Middle Tennessee State University, worked at the Davidson County Sheriff's Office and as Sales Counselor at ADS Security;

Craig Jenkins, B.S. in Business Administration, University of Tennessee, J.D., Nashville School of Law, assistant director taxpayer services at Tennessee Department of Revenue;

Ron Turner, B.A., Psychology, University of Central Florida, J.D., Vanderbilt University, Assistant Professor of Criminal Justice, Cumberland University;

Ms. Lynn Stinnett Williams, M.S. in Mass Communications from Middle Tennessee State University, Writer and Corporate Media Consultant, Lynn Williams Communications.

I started my service the next morning at a previously scheduled quarterly meeting between Mayor Bill Purcell and the school board at Antioch High School in my district. The latest figures on tax collections used to fund part of the school budget were presented, and since the budget was being constructed based on earlier projections on revenues, the mayor promised that any shortfalls in tax collections for schools will be covered by other sources and that the schools will be held harmless. I spent the rest of the week studying the proposed budget and consulting other stakeholders including the teachers' association, the Metropolitan Nashville Education Association [MNEA], and the Service Employees International Union [SEIU] which represents support staff in the schools, mostly school secretaries and custodians.

On April 23rd, 2002, at the first regularly scheduled meeting of the board, I took the oath of office, administered by Adolpho A. Birch, Jr., Justice of the Tennessee Supreme Court, the first of three times that Judge Birch performed this ritual for me within a fourteen-month period. In the next week, I also sent the following letter to members of the council:

" April 30, 2002.

Dear Councilman[Council Lady]:

This note is to thank you and the majority of your fellow Councilmen and Council Ladies who voted on 4/16/02 to appoint me to the vacant seat on the Board of Public Education.

That vote has sent a positive message to all segments of our community that Nashville is really a city that celebrates diversity. I will continue to spread that message while carrying out my duties on the Board with utmost diligence and on all other occasions such as high school graduation ceremonies, school assemblies and parent-teacher organization meetings which I expect to attend as a Member of the Board.

Yours sincerely,

Mebenin Awipi"

I have already mentioned that ten of eleven African-American members of the Council had voted for me. The eleven out of forty members was considered an even representation of the racial diversity of the city when only blacks and whites were considered. However, diversity was a little more than black and white [which was the topic of a speech that I made at a faculty meeting of the ITT Technical Institute years later as chair of the education Committee of the NAACP-Nashville Branch]. Nashville has several nicknames such as Music City USA for its country music industry, the Athens of the South for its six universities, Vanderbilt University and Peabody College of Education, Tennessee State University, Belmont University, David Lipscomb University, Fisk University and Trevecca Nazarene University; there is also Meharry Medical College. Nashville is also called the buckle of the bible belt for its religious book publishing industries. Because of its diverse economic foundation, it has attracted immigrants and refugees from various war-torn regions and the city has a full complement of Hispanics, Kurds, Southeast Asians from the Vietnam war era and later Somalis, Sudanese and Ethiopians, and of course, Nigerians. All these ethnic groups were reflected in our school population and it was always a pleasure to visit schools with special English Language Learners classes, and this is one of the most rewarding memories of my years of public service.

The three months of May, June and July 2002 were very busy months for our family and friends. As soon as the spring semester grades were submitted at Tennessee State University, I devoted all my time to serving diligently on the school board and running for a full four-year term, with the election scheduled for August 1, 2002. First, we sent out letters asking all my friends, fellow church members and the Nigerian-American community to contribute funds for the campaign. We attended events and meetings of the various Nigerian ethnic groups such as the Igbo Union, Egbe Omo Yoruba, Edo Union and Akwa Ibom Association. We received about five thousand dollars in contributions and my family made up whatever else we needed.

We also filled out questionnaires and attended interviews with three groups that sponsored political action committees to compete for endorsements. Of these, I earned the endorsement of the Chamber of Commerce Success PAC, a split endorsement from the Service Employees International Union (SEIU), and was rejected by the Teachers' union, Metropolitan Nashville Education Association (MNEA). The Success PAC endorsement came with a contribution of $2,500.00, the maximum amount allowed by the election finance law at that time, because they felt that I needed all the help I could get. There was also a free one-hour consultation with a local election consultant, attorney Harlan Dodson; accordingly, Yvonne and I spent about an hour and half with him on June 22, 2002 getting pointers on how we could conduct the campaign. Feedback from several members of the interview panel later informed me that my endorsement came after a long and heated argument, the main reason for opposing me being my chance for prevailing in the general election was an uphill battle and that they were reluctant to back a loser. The split endorsement from the SEIU came with a $1,000.00 contribution and instructions for any member of the organization who wished

to volunteer for me in the campaign, and several members did so. The main argument of the MNEA against me was that after observing me for several months, I was too much like the other members and that they were tired of nine-zero votes against their interests, and that my opponent was somebody who could listen to them and break the unanimous pattern.

It was obvious from both the Council election and the PAC endorsement debates that people did not give me much of a chance in the general election which was secret and people could vote according to their fears and prejudices without being called to account. There were three high barriers that I had to climb over. First, a large number of people could not pronounce my name MEBENIN. A secretary in the Central office, Melissa Bryant, after fielding many inquiries from radio and television reporters on how to pronounce it, came up with the analogy that it rhymed with a local town LEBANON; so on election nights, those reporting the results all got it perfectly, but those were professionals announcers who had taped and practiced on it. One friend joked that on the radio, she heard that I lost the election, but they pronounced my name perfectly.

Secondly, I still speak with my original Nigerian accent, so people noticed that first before they attempted to understand the content of my speech. Of course, I had been teaching electrical engineering courses for over twenty years by that time, but our students were used to various accents because the engineering faculty at TSU and many other American universities comprised heavily of foreigners like me from India, China, Korea and Middle Eastern countries. Besides, using mathematical expressions, equations and graphs written or displayed on blackboards, it was easy to communicate the contents of technical information. Finally, most people were aware that Nigeria is a country with a majority Muslim population, and there were frequent questions to my supporters asking whether I was a Christian or a Muslim. This was a great concern because the summer of 2002 was less than a year after the terrorist attacks of September 11, 2001, and there was heavy patriotism and fear of foreigners. My opponent's campaign flyers heavily capitalized on these factors, using the word "our" repeatedly to emphasize my outsider label. An example is the following opening statement in an advertisement in a community newspaper, The News Beacon: "We need leadership on the Metro Nashville School Board that knows what is happening in OUR schools" [with the 'our' capitalized and in heavy print.] It was true that by 2002, all my children were out of school [and two were already out of college at the University of Southern California and New York University, respectively] while my opponent's only child was in seventh grade in John F. Kennedy Middle School in our district; besides all my children had attended magnet schools outside our election district. Of course, throughout 2000 and 2001, I had visited all the schools in the district and knew a lot more than they were ever inclined to give me credit for, but they saw an advantage and exploited it fully. In rebuttal, I tried to highlight my superior academic and professional accomplishments, starting my flyers with the statement: "Our kids deserve the best! Quality education begins with the most qualified people on the School Board."

While campaigning for election, I also wanted to make sure that I did the most I could with the four months of tenure afforded by the Council vote. In those months, I participated in the work of passing both operating and capital needs budgets for the 2002-2003 school year. We also worked with the MGT school consultants to perform an audit of the physical conditions of all the schools in the city, which eventually documented the overcrowded state of many schools in my election district and guided the effort to build new schools in my district throughout my term of service. Finally, I attended the graduation ceremony at Antioch High School, held at the Grand Ole Opry music hall auditorium; as the representative of the Board of Education, I gave a short congratulatory speech and spoke the ritual sentence. "By the authority granted by the Metropolitan Nashville Board of Education and the State of Tennessee, I declare you graduates of Antioch High School, Class of 2002."

The main campaign activities were placing yard signs in visible street corners and front lawns of friends, advertisements in weekly community newspapers and mailing out thousands of postcards. In this first campaign, we used just two yard signs; one was about two feet by one and a half feet, with red and blue words on a white background, with the message: "Elect MEBENIN AWIPI SCHOOL BOARD DISTRICT 6 " and the slogan "Quality Education for Your $". The second sign was smaller, one and a half feet by one foot, with all red words on a white background, carrying the message " VOTE AWIPI School Board August 1, 2002".

By far the most labor intensive effort was the job of sticking address labels on post cards. The first batch of labels was for parents of students in the schools within my district, which was an incomplete list numbering about two thousands. From the feedback, we learned that sending out these cards was a good way to get our message to the voters. The next step was to obtain a disk of all registered voters in School District 6, numbering over thirty thousand, from the Election Commission. At that time, there was not a good filter to determine frequent or most likely voters, so we geared up to send a card to almost all the registered voters. At twenty-three cents each, the cost of postage alone was about seven thousand dollars, on top of the printing costs. However, knowing that we were facing an uphill battle, we decided to go with it. The first task was to print address labels from the information on the computer disk. A friend volunteered to perform this task for only the cost of materials. Joshua Gbasin was an immigrant from our same Izon/Ijaw tribe of Nigeria, running a small business as a mortgage broker and financial services provider; his company was named Friends and Associates and he used his computer resources to print tens of thousands of address labels for our campaign. We were able to send out more than twenty thousand cards; unfortunately, more than three thousand were returned because people had moved away and the election commission had not kept up their records. In many cases, the post office tried to forward the cards, but many did not leave forwarding addresses or the forwarding order had expired. Other reasons stamped on the returned cards were more intriguing: " RETURN TO SENDER- NO SUCH NUMBER"; or, "UNDELIVERABLE AS ADDRESSED". We hoped that enough of them were delivered to get our message across.

As stated earlier, our friends and fellow church members put in a great effort to send out these cards. We set up several tables in one room in our house that we call the pool room where people worked until late at night. A graduate student in the Electrical Engineering Department from Nigeria, Miss Seyi Olufiade, took batches of cards, labels and stamps home and organized other students to get it done. For those working in our house, my wife set out to provide refreshments and meals for the volunteers throughout the duration of the campaign. Among our friends were Ms. Eudith Williams, Miss Timinere Aboh, Dr. Edward Isibor and his wife Patience and Dr. Michael Ero, a former colleague at Bell Laboratories in Naperville, Illinois. Members of our church congregation were Brenda Nevels and her husband Harold Nevels, MD, Bob and Pam Jordan, Howard Forbes and his wife Digna Forbes, MD, Jeanne Campbelle-Kennedy, Linda Pegues Brinkley and JoAnn Treherne.

At last, the day of the election, August 1, 2002 arrived. Several friends volunteered to serve as poll watchers for me, carrying posters and urging those coming to vote to vote for me. I remember Brenda Nevels, Yvonne Sawyer and Elizabeth Kunnu spending the most time in this effort. When the polls closed, they were allowed to go to the election officials and obtain the results for that particular precinct. After seeing the numbers for three or four of the most busy precincts, we knew the election was lost. About a week later, we got the final totals from the August 8, 2002 News Beacon: "UNOFFICIAL RESULTS OF THE STATE PRIMARY AND COUNTY GENERAL ELECTION (AUGUST 1,2002)

SCHOOL BOARD 6

Mebenin Awipi 1,829

Lorinda Hale 4,593"

My opponent received nearly seventy-two percent of the vote to my twenty-eight percent, but this was not the end to my election story. In fact, I had the last laugh on her, because even though she got over seventy percent of the vote, I got to serve over eighty-five percent of the term of office that we had contested for. This is how it happened.

When the current version of the school board was created in 1964 as a result of combining the governments of Nashville City and Davidson County, the first members of the board were to be appointed by the mayor. To avoid having the mayor appointing his cronies to too many paid positions, it was decided that members of the board would not receive salaries, but would only be reimbursed for expenses up to $150 a month. As the job became more complicated during the years of school desegregation, it became a real sacrifice to serve on the board. Therefore in addition to a desire to serve the community, one had to be able to afford to serve; either one was self-employed as a professional or business owner, or one had to have an understanding employer. At the time I first started serving, the board consisted of four attorneys in private practice, a computer systems consultant, a supervisor in a venture capital company and two small business owners. Lorinda Hale, whose resume stated she had years of unspecified human resources experience, was thrust into this mix and it was a mismatch.

Since the board's work required a lot of communication, members were offered mobile phones with fixed minutes, and were responsible for usage beyond the limits of the group contract. Also, members who did not have health insurance from their workplace were allowed to join the group insurance program for certificated employees with full payment of the premiums without the subsidies that were available to employees. Lorinda signed up for family coverage, and on top of that the excess usage charges on her cell phone ran to over $900 a month. She very quickly fell behind in reimbursing the district for these expenses and soon resorted to the equivalent of check hiking practices. She also asked her friend Venn Denney, who had left the board to serve the district as director of student assignment services, for financial help in a manner that he thought was an attempt at influence peddling. He reported this to the legal authorities, and soon, damaging stories appeared in the newspapers. She resigned from the board early in February 2003 when faced with potential criminal investigation; she had served less than six months.

At this time, my family and I faced a dilemma. There were public and private calls for me to seek a return to the board. This time, if reappointed by the Metro Council, I could serve for six months before having to face a by-election in August 2003 for the remaining three years of the term of office which ran until August 2006. My wife's view was that my name and my accent had not changed, and that the majority of people were too prejudiced to vote in a secret election when they could not be called to account. My view was that even if I could serve only for six months, it was better than the four months that I had served previously, and that given a second chance, maybe people would overcome their prejudices and vote for me in sufficient numbers to win the election. After several weeks of soul-searching, I decided to seek the position again and submitted my name to the Metro Council. This was received with great humor and my supporters teased me that if I really wanted to serve on the school board, I must make sure to win the general election. As it turned out, there was no other candidate, so I was appointed to the board on an interim basis for the second time.

When I got back, after being sworn by Justice Birch for the second time on February 25, 2003, I was graciously welcomed back by the other board members, although I received some teasing for being AWOL for six months. Actually, I did not feel the absence because during that period, I had served on a Citizens Panel for a Community Report Card on the public schools. This report card was an accountability measure written into state and federal school improvement laws and the first was issued in 1993. The activity was sponsored by the Nashville Area Chamber of Commerce, and since their political action committee had sponsored me in the 2002 election, I thought it was a bit of payback to serve in this manner. The report I participated in generating was thus the tenth one. In the course of about three months, from September 2002 to January 2003, we had met weekly to study data and interview administrators to arrive at our progress report. I was therefore quite in touch with the school system in the six months that I was absent from the board. I was able to hit the ground running, to use a common slogan. After full participation in our discussions and decisions, I wrote a letter to the members of the Metro Council, thanking them for appointing me again, and summarizing the decisions made at the meeting and the votes I had cast in arriving at those decisions. This letter was very well received. First, they thought that after making many such appointments and confirmations to boards and commissions, they had never heard from the appointees again. Second, they were glad to receive some inside view of the working of the school board and its actions. Therefore, the chair of the board was asked to send a similar letter to the Metro Council after every board meeting, a practice that continued for two years, until a new council and board were elected.

After serving from February to April, 2003 it was time to decide whether to run in the by-election coming up in August 2003 to serve for the remaining three years of the term of office that started in August 2002. We were afraid of being rejected again, so I did not submit my nominating petitions to the election commission until very close to the deadline. When I finally did so, it was a relief to them because no one else had submitted to run and they were wondering whether they would have to extend the deadline. So it was that I ran unopposed in the by-election, which was quite a relief to me too. Unlike the previous year, I made only token effort this time. I needed only about one hundred votes to win, just in case there was a write-in contest. However, either as a good joke or in remorse for the previous year, I received three thousand and three hundred and seventy-five votes, and thus received the right to serve for another three years, until August 2006.

Another consequence of this episode was the decision to establish a salary for members of the school board. It became apparent that the conditions of serving on the board mitigated against achieving socioeconomic diversity among the members of the board. Diligent service required twenty to twenty-five hours of work a week: in addition to two meetings on the second and fourth Tuesday of every month, we had to read and study background documents relating to items on the agenda in order to make informed decisions. Also there were committee meetings, retreats and workshops, tenured faculty dismissal and student disciplinary hearings and attendance at community events and ceremonies such as school building dedications and citywide budget and political speeches. For example, I served at various times on committees dealing with the budget, capital needs (chair for two years), director evaluation, employee insurance, charter school applications evaluation and an ad-hoc committee on school choice. Therefore the necessary process was undertaken by a citizens group calling themselves "Friends of Public Schools", to pay school board members: a resolution was recommended by the Metro Charter Revision Commission; it was passed by the Metro Council and the issue was placed on the August 7, 2003 ballot as a charter amendment public referendum, and the referendum passed in the same August 2003 election in which I had run unopposed. Then the Metro Civil Service Commission had to recommend an amount, which came out to be fourteen thousand dollars a year [members of the Metro Council were being paid $17,000 a year] and a final enabling legislation was approved by the council in October 2003. This salary encouraged more working-class persons to run for election to the board in 2006, but only one was elected.

On Tuesday, August 26, 2003, Supreme Court Justice A.A. Birch administered the oath of office for the third time for me to start three more years of service on the board. With such unusual path to the office, I felt a particular obligation to serve diligently and that is what I endeavored to do. Over the four years, I attended over ninety-nine percent of the regular and special called meetings of the board; I missed one regular meeting due to illness, and one called meeting due to class conflict that I could not find a substitute for. Unfortunately, the special meeting was to vote on approval of the application for a charter school and the motion to approve failed on a four-four tie, so my absence was duly noted in the news reports. The Chamber of Commerce leaders were advocates for charter schools and were generally disappointed by my lukewarm support for charter schools in general, and this was just a case in point.

In fact, the charter school law in Tennessee was very restrictive in the view of their advocates. Most important was the requirement that these schools could only recruit students from failing public schools, and in 2004, the federal No Child Left Behind law had not been in operation long enough to label any of our middle schools as failing. Thus we rejected all middle school [grades 5-8] applications, even including the Knowledge Is Power Program [KIPP] that had strong national performance track record. In 2005, the law was changed to include students who were failing even if their schools were not. We have had a KIPP academy in our district since then and I was very supportive of their program while I was in office. Our first charter school was proposed by a Catholic nun and her sister who had a long track record of tutoring groups of disadvantaged students in some of the poorer sections of the city, and their K-4 school, the Smithson-Craighead Academy, had their charter renewed in 2007 for another five years. The particular charter school whose application had resulted in a tie vote on the board, The Nashville Academy for Science and Engineering was modeled after a similarly named one that had operated in Memphis for one year before the application was submitted in Nashville. It was supposed to start with a seventh grade class, and with the first version of the law, they could not recruit any students and we did not wish to approve a school without eligible students. Also, we did not think that the year's experience in Memphis was sufficient to prove that their concepts were successful in educating at-risk students. Lastly, there were no strong leading forces in Nashville to duplicate the founding leadership that was operating the Memphis school. So this application was denied the first year, and our action was upheld by the State Department of Education on appeal. Again, we rejected their application in 2005, but this time they prevailed on appeal to the State. We were then compelled to approve their application, but they could not open their school because they claimed that the approval came too late for them to make all the necessary arrangements. They were given a year's extension to start in fall 2006, they again failed to initiate operations and so their charter died.

My major legacy was construction of four new schools in the district that I represented. At the start, all the schools were overcrowded because the area had grown rapidly with a variety of residential developments. All the buildings were operating at up to one hundred and twenty-five percent of their designed capacities and there were dozens of portable classrooms taking up all available playgrounds and parking lots. As a member of the capital needs committee and as chairman in 2005 and 2006, we accelerated plans to construct two elementary schools, one middle school and started the construction of a high school. In fact, two months after

I had left office, I participated in the groundbreaking ceremony for the high school and I look forward to its dedication sometime in Fall 2008. According to our practice, these buildings will carry a small placard listing the names of all the sitting board members and some other elected city officials at the time of project funding approval. So my name will remain on these placards for as long as these buildings stay in use, which may be fifty to seventy years before they are totally torn down and rebuilt.

It was also the duty of the school board to approve names for our school buildings that would be inspiring to our students, parents and staff. We had a standing committee to make recommendations to the full board, but we always listened particularly to the wishes of the member representing the area where the school was located. We had guidelines including geographical features, national, state and local historic figures and those who made significant contribution to local education, provided they had been dead for a number of years so that no scandals were associated with their names. In our effort to accelerate construction of the first elementary school to alleviate dire overcrowding of two nearby schools, the project got under way before a name had been approved. When I returned to the board in 2003, the construction signpost simply stated "New Antioch Area Elementary School". We already had an Antioch Middle School and an Antioch High School, Antioch being the name of our section of the county. I thought we could complete the triple play by naming the new school "Antioch Elementary School" and recommend it to the committee. But many of my constituents were disappointed that the name was not creative enough. They circulated petitions suggesting other names including Johnny and June Carter Cash, the country music singers. However, they had not done anything in particular for public education, unlike Dolly Parton who had a foundation giving books to at-risk children every month until they started kindergarten. But going back to my profession of electrical engineering and my years of college and employment in New Jersey, I finally recommended the name "Thomas A. Edison Elementary School" and that proved to be a popular choice.

From this experience, when the time came to name three other schools, elementary, middle and high, I placed an advertisement in the community newspaper, The News Beacon, "Name Our Schools", listing two or three possibilities for each and asking the public to vote for their favorite names. The ballots were submitted to the district central office and tabulated by the executive director of facilities. The names approved for the schools were:

"A.Z. Kelley Elementary School", in honor of the first African-American parent to file a desegregation lawsuit against Davidson County after the Supreme Court's 1954 Brown V. Board of Education ruling outlawing separate but equal public schools;

"Thurgood Marshall Middle School" after the civil rights law who argued the case and later became a Supreme Court Justice;

"Cane Ridge High School", after the area where the school was originally intended to be located, and restoring the name of a school which was closed during the desegregation era.

Many of my critical actions on the board revolved around the Director of Schools, or what is called the superintendent of schools in many jurisdictions. The director of schools throughout my tenure was Dr. Pedro Garcia. He was hired in 2001 and since I was prepping to run for election, I followed the process carefully. He was not the board's first choice as the board had voted 5-4 to hire Dr. Carol Johnson, a highly reputed African-American educator who was then the superintendent of schools in Minneapolis, Minnesota; she was also a graduate of Fisk University in Nashville. However, some of the minority in that vote refused to accept the will of the majority as the rules called for and continued to bicker during the contract negotiation with Dr. Johnson. When she finally withdrew her candidacy, the terms that were worked out for her were offered to Dr. Garcia and he accepted.

By law, the director is the only employee that the board can hire, supervise and fire. In addition to providing oversight on the operations of the district, the board had to evaluate the director's performance, and by implication, that of the whole school district, and then vote annually on extensions of his contract. After two years of his tenure, it appeared to some of us that not much progress was taking place, particularly on closing academic performance gaps between African-American students and the other student groups; this was a high priority of the board and in particular to the three African-Americans on the board. However, we did not wish to encourage the type of musical chairs game that superintendents of schools were playing, going from one district to another, with an average tenure of less than three years at one sight. So after a long debate at a weekend retreat, we offered to extend his contract for another three years, but he had to guarantee staying for at least two years, with decreasing financial penalties for early departure to defray some of the cost of searching for a replacement. In spite of this clause, Dr. Garcia sought a similar position with Miami/Dade County in 2004, but was not hired. There were also rumors of a similar job search with The Los Angeles Unified school district in 2005. Meanwhile, the performance of our district was unsatisfactory, with the district as a whole and many individual schools not making Adequate Yearly Progress under the 2001 federal No Child Left Behind Law. So in 2005, with one year to go, I joined four other members who voted not to add another year to his contract, and to use the year as a probationary period before deciding whether to extend the contract further or to allow it to expire at the end of June, 2007.

Some members of the business community who were strong supporters of Dr. Garcia took great exception to this vote, and coupled with my lukewarm attitude towards charter schools, decided to target me for defeat in the August 2006 elections. Lucky for them, I had other barriers to overcome, so after a strenuous campaign, I lost my bid for reelection on August 3, 2006. The following were the final results:

"DAVIDSON COUNTY, TENNESSEE PRIMARY AND GENERAL ELECTION, AUGUST 3, 2006

SCHOOL BOARD DISTRICT 6

MEBENIN AWIPI	1811
DUANE N, DOMINY	721
KAREN Y. JOHNSON	2523."

In October 2006, the new board voted to extend Dr. Garcia contract for another three years. But with the poor performance of the school district becoming more plainly apparent, he was forced to resign in January 2008, taking a one year salary of $216,000 as a buyout.

In December 2006, I accepted a volunteer position as chairman of the education committee of the NAACP-Nashville Branch, in order to continue my involvement with public education in Nashville, Tennessee for a few more years.

2: TSU STUDENTS, 1980

CHAPTER TWO

Tennessee State University: 1985-2005

As I got close to finishing my doctoral studies at Columbia University in 1969, I applied for faculty positions at Historically Black Colleges and Universities [HBCUs] through the Southern Regional Education Board and received offers from Southern University in Baton Rouge, Louisiana and Prairie View A&M University in Texas. I also received an offer from the University of Lagos through a separate channel. However, I thought that I needed more real engineering experience beyond two summer jobs before undertaking to teach engineering in a university, so I accepted an offer from Bell Telephone Laboratories, Holmdel, New Jersey immediately after graduation. I hoped to teach in universities in the U.S.A. and Nigeria later in my career, and this hope was eventually fulfilled.

In 1979, after ten years of working at Bell Labs, I had an opportunity to explore my second career option. In those days, Bell Labs was really serious about employing a greater number of qualified African-American engineering graduates as part of their affirmative action program. As a means of raising their profile on the campuses which were producing these graduates while contributing to the quality of the faculty at these institutions, they started a visiting professor program in which members of the technical staff were loaned to an HBCU for an academic year. The International Business Machines company [IBM] and others also had similar programs. The best and brightest graduates would receive five or more job offers from competing high technology companies and government laboratories, so it was important to get our fair share of acceptances. It was an advantage for the future graduates to get to know black employees at the labs, so the few of us in those days were recruited to help recruit others like us. From 1974 to 1976, I served as part of the Bell System recruiting team at Howard University, which called for visiting the school almost every semester, getting to know the faculty and the best students who could qualify for Bell Labs by participating in seminars and providing equipment grants. Then in 1979, I applied to participate in the visiting professor program, hoping to serve at Southern University. However, a Nigerian-American, Dr. Edward Isibor, who had come to the USA on the same scholarship program as I did, was dean of the School of Engineering and Technology at TSU, and when my profile was circulated among the HBCUs, he decided to pick me to serve at his institution. So I spent the academic year 1979-1980 at TSU, commuting between Nashville and Naperville, Illinois where I had transferred from Holmdel. This was quite strenuous for me and my family, but Bell Laboratories was such a caring employer that we did not mind making sacrifices on their behalf.

Soon after I returned to Bell Labs in 1980, rumors started circulating about the breakup of the Bell System, including the breakup of Bell Labs into units serving the telephone operating companies [Bell Communications Research – Bellcore] and the research and manufacturing units, later called AT&T Bell Laboratories and Lucent Technologies, respectively. To avoid the period of instability, I decided to take up a teaching position at the University of Lagos, Nigeria, particularly since a democratic government had been established in 1979 following the Biafran Civil War of 1968-1972. In 1984, after the overthrow of the democratic government and establishment of another military government in Nigeria with laws being passed only by decrees, my family again decided to return to the USA, and I ended up as an associate professor of electrical engineering at TSU, starting in January, 1985. I will cover the stages of my life at Bell Labs and in Nigeria in other chapters.

Between the experiences at Howard University and TSU, I got to know the idea of Historically Black Universities and Colleges from the inside. Most of these were located in the Southern states of the USA, and they were mostly state-sponsored, and a few were private or sponsored by Christian religious denominations such as the Episcopalians [Anglicans], Methodists and Presbyterians. The city of Nashville has three of these HBCUs: Fisk University, founded by philanthropists in 1866 to educate freed slaves after the civil war; Meharry Medical College; and Tennessee State University, established by the state in 1912 as a separate institution for blacks. The latter was the most common reason for the establishment of all these institutions: for a hundred years after the emancipation of the slaves, the majority white population purported to practice "separate but equal" public education throughout the Southern States. However, while the separation part was easy to accomplish, the equality part was mostly a sham and these institutions were always forced to do more with less. In fact the white majority originally did not expect these institutions to produce professionals such as lawyers and engineers to compete with white professionals. The role that blacks were expected to play in the society of these Southern states was evident from the names of these institutions. They all had some additional descriptors such as Agricultural and Mechanical, A&M, Agricultural and Technical, A&T, and Agricultural and Industrial, A&I. TSU, for example, was founded as the Agricultural and Industrial Normal School, and was only intended to produce farmers, plumbers, electricians and teachers who could only teach at the separate black primary and secondary schools.

In spite of inadequate resources, the HBCUs educated the best and the brightest in the black population and built outstanding reputations in the professions and on the athletic playing fields. Examples from TSU included Olympic gold medal winners such as Wilma Rudolf, National Football League Super Bowl Most Valuable Player Richard Dent of the 1985 champion Chicago Bears, and Oprah Winfrey. Their alumni were also fiercely loyal to them.

After the US Supreme Court outlawed the practice of separate and unequal public education in 1954 in the case of Brown V. Board of Education, and after the Civil and Voting Rights Acts of 1965 and 1966, integration of the races at all levels of public education slowly began to take shape. At TSU, as at some other places, this led to the merging of formerly all black and all white schools, so that no school could be racially identifiable. It happened that while integration was good for the society as a whole, it was not so good for the formerly all-black institutions. The formerly all-white institutions were able to recruit the brightest and most talented blacks to their schools, but the formerly all-black institutions could not compete for the bright and talented blacks, and they could not recruit bright and talented whites either. This loss of talent was apparent to the general public in the athletic and sports arena, but the faculty was aware of it in the classroom as well, but nobody could talk about it comfortably and there was little that they could do about it. If the faculty complained to the administrators, they were told that if they did not like the students that the administrators recruited for their classrooms, then the faculty should go out and recruit their own students. Unfortunately, the workload of the faculty did not allow them to do much recruiting as the athletic coaches and assistant coaches did.

The politicians did their best by improving the facilities and other resources at these institutions, but the history prevented white students from embracing them wholeheartedly, and the black students rightly took advantage of the wider opportunities made available to them. We could observe these effects from the 1980s and 1990s but could only hope for a happy new equilibrium for coexistence among all institutions, whatever their historical foundation.

As stated earlier, the black graduates and the black community in general, are highly attached to these

HBCUs and are very protective of their continued existence. Those who were born in Africa and came to teach at these schools received much appreciation and friendship from the African-American community as fellow foot soldiers in the trenches of this social conflict. These institutions helped African-Americans to survive through an extremely trying period, from the end of the US Civil War in the 1860's to the achievements of the Civil Rights Movement in the 1960's, commonly known as the Jim Crow era, named after a popular character in minstrel shows in the 1800's. The doctors, dentists and lawyers trained through these institutions enabled African-Americans to construct a viable parallel universe of businesses, churches, professional organizations, fraternities and sororities in their segregated communities that ensured their survival through the darkest of days. African-Americans are afraid of letting these institutions disappear, in case they were needed again in the future.

The blacks are quite justified in this nagging fear, because in their experience, progress in racial integration and equal treatment has not been uniformly upward and forward; it has been quite simply a case of taking two steps forward and one step backward. When the British Empire outlawed the slave trade in 1832, the lives of the former slaves in their colonies became more bearable in a steady trajectory. Slavery continued in the United States through internal breeding to supply slaves to satisfy the demand, a system that was accompanied by all sorts of social injustices; when the male slaves did not cooperate by impregnating the females, the whites stepped in to do the job. For example, any child born to a female slave was considered a slave whether the father was a slave or not; in fact, the children of slave owners and their female slaves were slaves to their father, a situation that must have exerted severe psychological trauma to all parties, the children, the slave mother and the white fathers. Once classified as slaves, they were sold and abused as any other slaves. I have watched episodes on the Animal Planet channel in which lions and elephants have fought to the death defending their offspring. By not defending their own offspring, the slave owners were being less human than elephants and lions.

Whenever outsiders like me talk about slavery, the descendants of the slave owners are quick to say that slavery is over and that we should all forget about it. However, through their heritage societies, they want to remember the period of slavery as the golden age of their kind. It seems that what they want is a monopoly on history so that only their side of the story is told, but not the fact that their golden age was the worst nightmare for millions of others. Further, it is not yet over and the bad times are still rolling.

Also, one should acknowledge the progress that has taken place since the passing of the Civil Rights and Voting Rights Laws of 1965 and 1966. Many of the overt forms of segregation and discrimination were eliminated, but of course laws do not change people's hearts, so a lot of racism simply went underground. When federal courts ordered the desegregation of public schools, religion-based schools such as Catholic schools were exempted in respect for the separation of church and state. Using this as a loophole, the opponents of desegregation started numerous "Christian" schools which were also exempted from the desegregation orders. Thus the name of Christianity was used blasphemously to spite their neighbors, a far cry from the directive to love your neighbor as yourself. This was done in spite of the clear lesson of who your neighbor is: your neighbor is not someone that looks like you, thinks like you or worships like you. Your neighbor is some one who is different in one or more of the above characteristics. There is thus a lot more progress needed, with the ultimate goal being absolute equality, such that all achievement is determined by individual merit and there would be no statistical correlation between race or ethnicity and all socioeconomic factors such as educational achievement, income or criminal behavior and incarceration rates.

Even today, those of us who came voluntarily from Africa are still puzzled by the commonly accepted classification of any child born to a white and a black parent as black. Whenever I have had an occasion to express this confusion, I am reminded of the "one drop of black blood rule" which states that you are black if you have a drop of black blood in your veins. Unfortunately, there is no corresponding "one drop of white blood" rule, or fifty. This treats black blood as a "stain" and feeds into irrational and racist attitudes.

Of course, I also find the detailed classification of mulattos, quadroons, octoroons, et cetera used in Brazil and other places as distasteful. Up to today, the one drop rule is having a toll on people's lives. I have a good friend who was born out of wedlock to a woman who might have been no more than one quarter black, and a white man. This is known because after the death of her adoptive parents, she spent many years searching, and found her biological parents. As an adult, this friend is indistinguishably white, but as a baby, judging only from her mother, she was classified as black, and was adopted by a black family. She has therefore lived as a black woman, attended TSU and married a black man. She just describes herself as a fair skinned black woman [and I am thinking a very fair one indeed!] But it does not affect our friendship, as I have many white friends, from neighbors to fellow TSU faculty members and some who served with me on the school board. However, in one of my friend's work places, her white co-workers thought she was white and treated her as such, inviting her to have lunch with them and so on. But when her daughter came to visit her at the workplace, they realized that she was "black", and their attitude towards her changed. She did not stay at that workplace for long after that. Of course, everybody has issues of personal identity, but I was sorry that my friend was saddled with an extra burden because of society's shortcoming in race relations and labeling. In addition to trying to answer the "Who am I" question as everyone else, she and others like her have to also answer an "What am I" question.

What I wish to see is a classification that makes sense biologically or necessary for sociological and demographical purposes, instead of what was useful for the perpetuation of the system of slavery in the US southern states. Society could decide on a fully matrilineal system, or especially with the reliability of DNA testing, on a patrilineal system. In a matrilineal system, everybody's race will be consistently determined by the race of the mother if there is any difference between the races of the father and mother. If the mother is European, then the child is European, and if the mother is African, then the child is African. Under such a simplified system, Barack

Obama would be European and Tiger Wood would be Asian; Tiger Wood's daughter would be European since her mother is Swedish. This will save a lot of children from racial identity crises and could go a long way towards making race less relevant in US society.

The other side of the coin to very white looking people being classified as black is to have very black people being classified as white. While affirmative action was being taken seriously, we had the ironic situation at TSU where the whites were considered the minority, therefore all employment decisions had to show that qualified whites were given a fair opportunity to apply and be considered for the position. In the Affirmative Action addendum to employment offers, it happens that all those from the subcontinent of India were classified as white. But those from the southern tip of India were quite black in complexion. Therefore it was always disturbing to our clerks and administrative assistants to prepare these documents in which persons that were darker in complexion than them were being called white and they were called black; they were just struck by the absurdity of such classifications, as they were in many other places.

Again, on a personal note, even though I am aware that no classification system is ever perfect, some are less destructive than others. One system that is fair and neutral for the United States is to do away with the use of colors and use the ancestral continent as a hyphen. The African-Americans have started the ball rolling by rejecting the color label, since there was such a range of colors in their communities. While the original Africans were black, those that are really black are now a minority;

most are in different shades of brown, so it would be inaccurate to call them all black. The original purpose of the black and white designations was an act of linguistic chauvinism to claim superiority of the slave owners over their slaves. Since the Africans were black, the Europeans wanted to select a color for themselves that created the most distance between them and the slaves. Even though their faces were only pale under special circumstances, they chose the color white for themselves, knowing that white is opposite to black, just as good is to evil and truth is to falsehood. For those who remember bits of their high school physics class, the skin color of most persons of European descent is yellowish-orange on the solar spectrum, with wavelengths between 620 and 630 nanometers.

So one step towards removing the remnants of the slavery system is to call people European-Americans, Asian- Americans, Native-Americans and African-Americans. The Native-Americans, who were originally called Indians by the Europeans, were happy to have their name corrected since there was a very big ocean between their land and India. It is clear that nobody was happy with being described by a color: the Europeans did not like being called Pale Faces, the Natives did not like the label Redskins and the Asians did not like being called Yellow Skins. In fact, no group of people likes to call themselves or have others call them by a name based upon some physical characteristic of the group, no matter how admirable that trait may be. We cannot imagine any group being happy to be called Slant Eyes, Thin Lips or Fat Buttocks. Human beings are made of such complex variations of physiological and psychological characteristics that being labeled by any one of them is invariably demeaning and insulting.

Of course, other languages have some chauvinistic traits as well. In my tribal language, we use the term "IZON" to mean "true" or "the real deal". For example, "IZON YE" means the truth, or "IZON KEME" means a good man.

So the up and down nature of racial progress has played a role in black attitudes. As I came to understand it, right after emancipation and during reconstruction after the civil war, blacks acquired some fair level of social and political equality, but this was brutally suppressed after the end of federal occupation. Again, after the civil rights movement of the 1960s, there was school integration and affirmative action in the 1970s and 1980s leading to a fair amount of social and economic progress for the black population, but a more conservative US Supreme Court began to tear down these programs as quotas and so in the first decade of the 21st Century, it is not clear which direction the fight for equality will be taking in the foreseeable future. That is the reason the National Association for the Advancement of Colored People [NAACP] currently uses the slogan "Still Your NAACP, Still As Needed Now As Ever".

After living in New Jersey, New York and Illinois for my first twenty years in the US, I was not so sensitive to the racial factor as I came to be when I started to live in Nashville, Tennessee. Unknown to me, even my getting hired had to go through a racial balancing filter. TSU had just absorbed a previously white school, the University of Tennessee at Nashville [UTN] in the early 1980s. For the school of engineering, the black dean of engineering at the previously black TSU was appointed Dean of the merged school. The previous white dean of UTN refused to serve under the black dean and resigned, and all the white faculty followed his example. So the new TSU was under pressure to hire white faculty to provide racial balance. Therefore, the dean was told that he could not hire me, a black man, unless he also hired a white faculty member as well. So a white assistant professor of electrical engineering was hired at the same time that I was hired. The student body was about eighty percent black and the faculty consisted of three Indians, two whites and later one Bangladeshi and one Syrian. As it turned out, the white fellow hired at the same time left after two years, and I served for twenty years because for me, it was not just a job; it was also partly a mission as well.

Teaching at TSU as a permanent fulltime faculty member was quite different from being a Bell Labs visiting professor. As a Bell Labs employee, I could get all my supplies and other needs from the Labs and the resources of the Bell System. For example, one of the courses that I taught on both situations was communication systems engineering. During my visit, I was able to work with the public relations departments of the Labs and the Bell operating company serving Nashville, South-Central Bell, to obtain access to secure locations and show my students the central office transmission and switching equipment embodying the principles I was teaching them in class. A group photograph of me and my students along with a story about the visiting professor program was published in the South-Central Bell employee newsletter and the Bell Labs monthly employee magazine, The Bell Labs Record. But as a full-time TSU employee, I did not have similar access, and there was also the complication of the breakup of the Bell System which was in effect by 1985.

In the early period of my tenure, I taught courses in electric circuits, communication systems and electronics. As younger and inexperienced faculty members were hired, we assigned them to teach courses closest to their areas of expertise, and the older faculty migrated to teaching other courses, particularly at the undergraduate level; hence in the latter part of my stay, I taught courses in electromagnetic theory, digital communications and computer communication networks. As the technology was rapidly developing, we had to constantly revise the contents of our courses in order to prepare our students to cope with what they could be assigned to design five or ten years into their careers, but also to hold their own on design teams consisting of graduates from all the other outstanding engineering schools in the country. It was therefore very important that our students be capable of learning to learn continuously after graduation, whether in formal graduate studies or through in-company workshops and seminars. To best prepare them for this role, we had to teach them fundamental principles which could be modeled and described by mathematical analysis. The students therefore had to be competent in mathematics to the level of trigonometry and calculus before embarking on engineering studies, but this proved to be a severe stumbling block for many students. Thus a nominal four-year program took six or seven years, and of course the students were frustrated at this protracted effort and even after meeting all requirements, the competence of the graduates was questionable because they had forgotten much of what was learned earlier.

As every teacher and professor knows, the better your students are, the easier and more rewarding your job becomes. Good students not only make you look good as a teacher by learning so much on their own, but you also learn from them from the questions they ask and the projects they undertake. For example, while guiding two master's degree candidates on their terminal projects, we ended up writing and publishing conference papers, one dealing with the signal to noise effects of digital filtering with or without band limiting analog filters ahead of sampling the analog signal. The second paper analyzed the effect of applying Bessel functions in place of sinusoidal functions in digital representation of speech signals in the frequency domain. The first student transferred to Vanderbilt University after earning the master's degree from TSU and with the confidence gained as a published author, went on to complete his Ph.D. degree with honors and acclaim.

With good students, our relations with the students were also much more comfortable since you do not have to worry about awarding failing grades, which is always painful to both teacher and student. In the late 1980s and early 1990s, while our children were young, several of my students served as babysitters for us, and sometimes as house sitters as well when both my wife and I had to travel out of town. Two sisters, Jacquelyn and Cynthia Prewitt, performed this service for us until their graduation and they remained good friends to our children for years after.

We also did our best with those students who had difficulty with the content of our curriculum because we were aware that electrical engineering could be a difficult subject, especially if the student was not strong in the prerequisite science and mathematics courses. Qualifying as an engineer could make a big difference in their future earnings; for example, at some point in the middle 1990s, an electrical engineering graduate earned a starting salary of over forty thousand dollars while an elementary education graduate would start with twenty thousand dollars. Also, sometimes we had the proverbial C student doing very well later in their careers, so we were always hoping to produce such "diamonds in the rough". Of course, even if they might not be good electrical engineering students, they were still good individuals and we tried to help them in their quests as much as we could.

So it was a labor of love as well as a job for twenty years. As I have stated earlier, the relation between African immigrants to the US, who sometimes call themselves American-Africans and the African-Americans who have descended from those who came here originally as slaves is a sensitive one, as both sides have had trouble understanding the other. Since the days of independence of African colonies from European empires, Africans and African Americans have worked to solve common problems. For example, the NAACP has had international programs which have impacted black people in Africa and the Caribbean region, particularly in the fight against apartheid in South Africa.

When I decided to retire in 2005, it was due to a combination of personal and professional reasons. Early retirement was always a goal of mine, and at age sixty-four, I was half-way between the minimum age of sixty-two that qualified for collecting social security benefits and the age of sixty-six when there would be no penalty in benefit amount. I was also critical of people who stayed on the job long after their professional effectiveness had diminished and I wanted to avoid a similar situation by lingering on the job.

3: WITH IZON STUDENTS AT
UNIVERSITY OF LAGOS, 1983

CHAPTER THREE

Lagos And Port Harcourt, Nigeria: 1981-1984

This chapter will cover our experiences while I worked as a professional in Nigeria squeezed between the periods of employment at Bell Laboratories and Tennessee State University. Furthermore, this brief period was about evenly divided between serving as a Senior Lecturer in Electrical Engineering at the University of Lagos and serving a dual role as Director of a Center for Special Projects and Reader at the University of Science and Technology, Port Harcourt, Rivers State, which was my home state at the time before the creation of Bayelsa State in the Federation of Nigeria.

In 1981, when it became clear that the Bell System would be broken up into a variety of companies and that employment at Bell Laboratories would undergo a period of instability and uncertainty, I decided to seek employment in Nigeria. In addition to fulfilling an earlier promise to serve in Nigeria in return for the scholarships to study in the USA, I also wished to act on a desire to enable my children to become familiar with the country of origin of both their parents. In 1981, they ranged in age from eight years to one year and we thought it was a reasonable age to let them experience a new culture. Our children were born while we were living in New Jersey and Illinois as permanent resident aliens and since they were US citizens, we expected that they would live their adult lives in the USA. As first generation immigrants, we thought we should provide the knowledge they would need when the time came for them to ask the inevitable questions of "Who am I and where did I come from?" My wife's mother, their maternal grandmother had lived with us for a number of years in New Jersey and Illinois, so they had had a little contact with Nigerian culture through her as well, but we still wanted to do more if we could. As advocates of student travel will testify, living in another culture is an educational experience at any age and this move could generate an advantage that they would carry with them throughout their lives. My wife and I both speak the Izon tribal language with different accents, but we had not made any particular effort to enable our children to speak Izon as well. They had picked up a little understanding from their grandmother, but we hoped they would pick up more while in Nigeria.

I had left Nigeria in 1962 to study in the USA, and had visited for two weeks in 1972. Going back in 1981 was quite a strange experience. First, physically moving the family from one country to the other had to be done in stages. Even though my wife had grown up in Lagos, we had no home to go back to, and this was something we hoped to establish during our stay. So I had to go by myself alone to establish a temporary residence with the assistance of the University. This was a process that they were quite good at since so many of their faculty had studied outside the country and had returned in the same way that I was then undertaking. For example, the Dean of the Faculty of Engineering was a graduate of Cornell University; among my fellow lecturers in the Electrical Engineering Department were graduates of University of California at Berkeley, the University of Maryland and my friend Dr. Abiodun Kassim who attended Princeton University as an undergraduate and received his terminal degree from Ohio University, Athens. In fact, because of their assistance, they were quite unhappy when I left after only two years of employment there.

After I had secured my employment paperwork, I returned to the USA and packed our belongings as much as we could and then transported the whole family on Nigerian Airways which was operating two direct flights a week between New York and Lagos at that time. The tickets were provided by the University and were good only on Nigerian Airways. We were late from the connecting flight from Chicago, so we could not secure seats for our family, but our luggage was taken to Lagos ahead of us. We were given a room at the International Hotel at the JFK airport, and spent three days as tourists again in New York before catching the next flight to Lagos. Much to our pleasant surprise, our luggage was bundled in a corner of the arrival area, with the only damage being incurred by our baby's crib.

When we told our friends, they offered several possible explanations for the unusually good behavior of the airport baggage handlers. Some thought that since our luggage was mostly children's stuff, they knew we were a Nigerian family returning with children who had been born abroad and they were eager to welcome us and show their best side. Also, some pieces showed that we were headed for the premier university in town and they were happy that we were coming to share our knowledge with future generations of Nigerian leaders. As many visitors to Nigeria are aware, the love of children is one of the saving graces of Nigerian people. The indigenous tribe in Lagos, the Yorubas, have a special name for children born abroad; they call them "Tokumbo" whether they are male or female, and they always give twins the names Taiwo and Kehinde, in the order of birth, which to me is demonstration of their general love of children. Of course having many children was an advantage in earlier times when the high birth rate was to balance a Malthusian high infant mortality rate. But when improve healthcare reduced the mortality rate while the behavior of high birth rate was unchanged, there was a population explosion that is still dogging the economy and social services.

Lagos is the poster city for human population overwhelming civil infrastructure. On the roads and streets, dust in the dry season and floods and potholes in the rainy season are the rule everywhere. The conventional wisdom was that American cars could not stand up to the poor road conditions so we did not ship any car home when we returned. We were used to the condition in the US where with a good job and credit, you could buy a car to meet your family's transportation needs. Starting a month after starting employment at Bell Laboratories, I got a 1968 Mustang convertible. As the family grew, we added a 1972 Chevy Nova. Then as the family grew again, we traded the Mustang for a full-size Ford LTD, As we were planning to go back, we sold the LTD and bought a Dodge Aspen. So for the majority of the time, we had two cars in the family to shuttle the kids to school and other events as well as working at different locations. We thought we could do the same in Lagos. However, that was a big mistake since you could only get a loan from your employer or bank loans had to be guaranteed by the employer or government. Our application was put on a long waiting list and it was through my wife's employment with Lagos State government that we were able to get a car after almost four months.

In the US, we were both used to driving cars with automatic transmission, but the most commonly available cars in Lagos were equipped with stick shift. We had to learn fast how to operate such a car, and as we did so, we destroyed several clutches before we became proficient at it. Driving on the streets of Lagos also took some time to get used to. At almost all intersections, there were no traffic lights, so merging into moving traffic was quite an art, requiring a quick entry into the smallest gap between cars, using first gear. In addition, due to flooding and potholes, one could not stick to a traffic lane but had to swerve and zigzag around pools and obstacles along the way, frequently getting into the lane for opposing traffic.

The University of Lagos was founded in 1961, immediately following the country's independence in 1960. Lagos was the

federal capital at that time and the university was intended to join three other comprehensive universities [at Ibadan, University of Nigeria at Nsuka and and Ahmadu Bello University at Zaria] to produce advanced degree graduates to serve as faculty members at the increasing number of new state and privately sponsored institutions. However, in the two years I served there, the electrical engineering department awarded only one doctoral degree and the recipient was already a lecturer at our department. Less technical fields might have been more successful in producing advanced graduates, but most engineering departments still relied on foreign trained Nigerians to fill their faculty rosters.

In the early 1980s, there were less than ten universities for a country of over one hundred million in population, so competition for admission into the universities was very fierce and the University of Lagos was able to select the top of the crop for admission. Accordingly, the caliber of students was very high. Since the quality of secondary education was still quite high after twenty years of independence, our students in engineering were very capable. As I was informed by my colleagues, the state of development of the country determined the popularity of the various engineering specialties. Civil engineering was the most popular, followed by mechanical engineering. I was used to having electrical engineering being the most popular in the USA in the 1960s to the 1980s, so it was a realty check to be a distant third. However, I taught the two semester sequence of introductory electrical circuits and electronics courses which was required for all engineering majors, so I saw the full spectrum of the student body at their second year level. I was quite impressed by their academic accomplishments and diligence.

Before we left the US, we took care of the children's vital documents to protect their rights as citizens. They were all issued US passports, and when we arrived in Lagos, they were registered at the US Embassy as US citizens living with their parents in Nigeria. Even though they were still minors, they were included in the emergency evacuation plan for US citizens in case of civil disorder and the breakdown of law and order. They were assigned to an embassy staff member as an emergency contact and this staff member was responsible for knowing where they were at all times in case they had to be picked up in a hurry. They made monthly visits to our house to observe them and drop off reports on the security status of the country, which I found quite interesting. In fact, later in 2000 after we had all returned to the US and both my wife and I had become naturalized citizens, my wife spent a year in Ethiopia and experienced the same treatment. I also visited for two weeks and attended a Memorial Day reception at the US Embassy in Addis Ababa at which we were given a security briefing since there was an ongoing conflict between Ethiopia and Eritrea at the time. What they told us was that in case of riots and siege of the embassy gates, we should not try to get into the embassy because the marines would barricade the gates and would not open them for anyone.

When I left Nigeria in 1962, the country was divided into three political regions, each with a premier as head of government and a legislature. There was the Northern Region with headquarter at Sokoto, the Western Region with headquarter at Ibadan, and the Eastern Region with headquarter at Enugu. A few years later, a Midwestern Region was created with headquarter at Benin City. The federal government was located at Lagos. After independence, my native part of the Niger Delta was in the Western Region and the other part of the Delta was in the Eastern Region. The boundary between the regions was drawn along what was thought to be the main channel of the Niger River after it had split into more than a dozen creeks and channels before emptying into the Atlantic Ocean. The conventional wisdom was that the European colonizers who partitioned Africa in the nineteenth century did not understand or consider tribal or ethnic affiliations of the native populations when they drew up National boundaries in Berlin. So Yorubas were split between Nigeria and Dahomey [named Benin after independence from France]. The Hausas were split in the Sahel region below the Sahara Desert between Nigeria, Chad and Niger.

In drawing regional boundaries before independence, the Ijaws [Izons] were now split between Western and Eastern Regions and later, between Western, Midwest and Eastern Regions. A large group of people were thus condemned to be minorities in three political subdivisions. The Northern Region was dominated by Hausas and Fulanis, with significant groups of minorities around the Jos Plateau and Benue districts. The Western Region was dominated by Yorubas, with Izons as minorities. The Eastern Region was dominated by Igbos, with Izons, Efiks and Ibibios as minorities. In Nigeria, and in Africa generally, minorities have hardly ever been treated well, and even though the creation of many more states made the situation much better, the unrest in the Niger Delta has persisted to this day.

The tensions and conflicts between the regions led to countervailing military takeovers of the government in 1966 and the Biafran Civil War from 1967 to 1970. After the civil war, it was thought that more states should be created so that minorities could receive a better deal in the context of the Nigerian Federation. It started with twelve states and the federal territory around Lagos, but more states were created until we now have thirty-six states and the federal territory around Abuja.

This short review of Nigerian political history is to explain why I spent the next two years in Port Harcourt, Rivers State. My native clan of the Niger Delta was situated in Rivers State when I returned in 1981. As soon as I settled in Lagos, I received a string of visits from relatives and hometown friends who thought I could be more useful and have a bigger impact if I came to work at the newly established Rivers State University of Science and Technology [RSUST] instead of being at the University of Lagos. They also pointed out all the political connections that I could take advantage of in my work at UST. I had briefly been introduced to the state governor, Melford Okilo, while he was a member of the federal parliament in 1962 and he had acted as one of the references for my passport and visa applications prior to leaving for study in the USA. Then in 1968, during the civil war and while I was a graduate student at Columbia University, we had met again at a party around the United Nations. The majority whip in the state assembly was also from my hometown, along with some special assistants to the governor and the secretary to government, the latter being similar to the chief of staff to the governor.

I was flattered but skeptical, since I could not predict how long we were going to be in Nigeria and my wife was certainly more comfortable in Lagos where she had grown up and had many friends. As I stated above, UST was just being upgraded from a technical institute to a

University and I was appointed to the Governing Council [equivalent to the board of trustees] representing my local government area. This required going to Port Harcourt every quarter for all-day meetings overseeing the operation of the university.

Thus I got to know the institution and its leadership quite well. The vice-chancellor [equivalent to the president of a US university], Professor Turner T. Isoun, was a graduate of Michigan State University, and a native of Odi in Yenagoa Local Government Area. The registrar, Mr. M.B. Mieyebo was from Bomadi, where I had completed my primary education and where I had taught at St. Brendan's Catholic high school for six months prior to going to the USA in 1962. I also had several relatives working at different levels at the university and all urging me to come on down.

I thought it would be a new experience working among friends and relatives and to share whatever positive outcome from our work with people closer to our hearts. In contrast, whereas I had very loyal friends at the University of Lagos, I was still quite an outsider among the majority Yorubas who constituted the power hierarchy at the institution. The then head of the electrical engineering department, late Professor Seriki, whom I had met in Monterey, California in 1968 at the Asilomar Conference, and my fellow Princeton graduate, late Dr. Kassim, made every effort to get me to feel at home. But the Yorubas had their own kinship lines that I was clueless about. Their clans were divided into Egbas, Ijebus and Ekitis which they recognize from names, accents and hometowns. Not knowing all of this, my friendships crossed lines that made people feel

I would not be a reliable ally in bureaucratic infighting. At RSUST, I would be part of the majority ethnic group and it would be easier to know who was what, so I would not inadvertently offend people out of ignorance.

So in January 1983, I accepted a position as Director of the Centre for Special Projects [CSP] at RSUST. This was a very responsible position since a lot was expected of the Centre. The founders of the university wanted to ensure that it was not just an ivory tower, but would be engaged in the technological development of the state. The law establishing the university has the following goals for CSP:

" SECOND SCHEDULE

1. (a) The Centre for special projects shall engage the talents and facilities of all the disciplines in the   University through the execution of various joint projects of special relevance to the State and country.

    (b) The centre shall deal with projects internal and   external to the University and thus provide links with the private sector."

With this mandate, and while also retaining my seat on the governing council and holding a joint appointment as Reader in electrical engineering, I held a unique place in the university hierarchy. It also took some legal clearance for me to be a political appointee on the council and be a full time employee of the university; the other members of the council by statute included the vice-chancellor and four members elected by the faculty senate, but I was the only political appointee. I was cleared to serve, but it just added to the jealousy and envy of some rival groups who thought the Central Izon community had too much authority at the university. We were able to withstand these pressures as long as we had close support from the governor's office.

The Centre had inherited a farm, a mechanical workshop, a bookstore and a campus restaurant from the technical institute days and we tried to add new activities such as a food processing plant. This required foreign exchange transactions to pay for some equipment from France, and at that time, foreign exchange was a sensitive subject.

One way that I utilized those political connections that they had promised was to publish three opinion pieces in the state owned newspaper called The Tide. After the 1982 Falklands War between Argentina and Great Britain, I thought the most effective weapon the Argentine forces employed against the invasion fleet were the Exocet missiles. But these were imported from France, and once hostilities occurred, the French were no longer willing to sell them and the British and US fleets established a blockade on further military imports. So the Argentine forces did not have enough missiles in stock and did not have the manufacturing capacity to produce them as they were needed. I pointed out in my piece that Third World countries should learn a lesson that they should not expect to win wars using only imported weapons in stock, but must endeavor to establish vertically integrated manufacturing capacity for the weapons critical to national security. By vertical integration, I meant that security must include supply and processing of raw materials such as petroleum and steel, but also supporting heavy machinery industry. As a fan of World War II movies and television programs, I was aware that the US won the war by out-producing Germany and even the Germans had run out of gasoline in the Battle of the Bulge. So I advised that establishing a university of science and technology was not enough without adequate training facilities for technicians and skilled craftsmen. This was a lesson that I had also learned from Bell Laboratories.

During elections, it was popular for all politicians in Nigeria to promise rapid economic development and industrialization of the district, state or country. The first step was manpower development which was accomplished by establishing universities and granting scholarships for students to study science and technology in advanced countries. This was a correct step. The problem was that when these trained persons returned and told the politicians what to do, their message was not welcome any more. The skilled manpower needed an adequate infrastructure of water supply, reliable electricity service and good transportation and communication services. The politicians enjoyed using these programs for outrageously inflated contracts that feed their graft and greed. I thought the corruption had no limits since the appetites were insatiable. Whether a powerful politician acquired a million dollars, one hundred million or billions, it never seemed to be enough. I thought this was due to the practice of polygamy and the resulting large and extended family obligations that the powerful members of society incurred. Of course polygamy was considered a religious obligation by Muslims in Nigeria, and many of the tribal customs allowed in, with only a minority of Christians practicing real monogamy. Needless to say, proselytizing against polygamy was a very unpopular activity in the state and other parts of the country.

In 1984, Nigeria sent a good contingent of athletes to the Summer Olympic games in Los Angeles. Since the Soviet block boycotted these games in retaliation for the US boycott of the Moscow games in 1980, competition was less intensive and the Nigerians won a number of medals. Still, there were spectacular failures on the part of others that people had thought were outstanding. The lesson that pointed out was that there was a difference between local and global excellence. I even used one of my nieces as an example when she thought she did well by being near the top of her class in high school but did not fare well in the West African School Certificate national examination. I advised people to be more realistic in self assessment by using national and global standards of excellence. For example, the world and Olympic records for men's one hundred meters dash was under ten seconds, so we should not expect much if we sent an athlete whose best time was over eleven seconds. When my niece turned forty, with a family of three children, I gave her a copy of this piece and we had a good laugh over it.

In August 1983, a second set of elections were held at the expiration of the terms of office for those elected in 1979 to establish a civilian government after the long tenure of

various military governments since 1966. I was able to register and cast a vote in the presidential election in Lagos and wanted to vote in the state elections for governor in Port Harcourt since I had dual residence in the two states. However, I missed the deadline and when

I expressed my disappointment to a friend, he asked me whom I would have voted for. I said I had wanted to vote for Okilo, and he said that I should not worry and that it had taken care of. I was disgusted with that and as it turned out, Okilo was declared the winner with about ninety percent of the vote. That was the common outcome for all the elections that year: almost all incumbents claimed to have won with outlandish majorities.

Unfortunately, in December 1983, the military declared that the elections had been fraudulent, and took over control of the government again. This had now become common practice in Nigeria and some other African countries. They dismissed all the elected officers, suspended the constitution and appointed military and police officers as governors of all the states. New laws were made by decrees and made to be retroactive to any date they wished. Living under this type of military dictatorship was new to me whereas others had been through that experience since 1966. We survived for a year, and then decided that it was time to go back to the USA and that is how we ended up in Nashville, Tennessee in 1985.

4: BELL LABS PR PHOTO, 1972

CHAPTER FOUR

Bell Telephone Laboratories: 1969-1981

In July 1969, after I had met all requirements for the Doctor of Engineering degree at Columbia University, I accepted a position as a Member of the Technical Staff at Bell Labs in Holmdel, New Jersey. As stated earlier, I had received offers of teaching positions from Southern University, Prairie View A&M University and the University of Lagos. I had also attended job interviews with the Communications Satellite Corporation in Washington, DC and the General Electric Electronics Division in Syracuse, New York, but received no offers from either of them. So Bell Labs was the only opportunity to acquire some industrial engineering experience before possibly changing to a teaching career and it was an ideal opportunity.

The Bell Labs that I served was significantly different from the Bell Labs of today, even though there has obviously been an effort to retain the name as a brand. The Bell Labs that existed then could not exist without the Bell System that supported it. After the breakup of AT&T in the 1980s, the employees scattered into three units: Lucent, Bell Communication Research, [BellCore], and AT&T Bell Labs. All three units have since been acquired or have merged with other companies to the extent that it is not easy to recognize the bulk of the original organization. The former employees who retired or joined other companies and universities act just like an alumni group of a beloved university and love to reminisce about the good old days. Unfortunately, what is good for one group may not be good for others. However, in this case, the problem was not with Bell Labs, but with the monopoly exercised and sometimes abused by the Bell System. Bell labs had the resources and the critical mass in manpower and talents to generate innovations in communication technology, but the rate of implementation of technology was not only limited by normal market forces of supply and demand, but sometimes by the monopoly desire to protect past capital investments which by regulation was being depreciated over a forty-year period. Thus while a product such as the picture phone died for valid market reasons, the treatment of data communication devices to protect the network was far in excess of technical reason.

Bell Labs in the 1970s was organized into vice-presidential areas as follows:

Area 10: Research [mostly chemistry, physics and mathematics];

Area 20: Electronic Devices and Materials [solid state and integrated circuits];

Area 30: Customer Equipment [telephones, data and business terminals];

Area 40: Transmission Systems [local loop and carrier systems];

Area 50: Switching Systems [local central office, toll switches, electronic switches and operator services including traffic service position systems];

Area 60: Military Systems;

Area 70: Employee Benefits;

Area 80: Financial Administration;

Area 90: Business Information Systems.

Under each vice-president, there were three or four executive directors with two-digit labels such as 31, 32, or

33 in area 30. Then under each executive director were several directors with labels such as 331,332 and so on. Under the directors were department heads with four-digit labels. So the department I started out came to be 3325 which was attached to several documents generated during my service.

To be employed as an engineer, called a member of Technical Staff [MTS], we were recruited by volunteer technical staff at our campus and if we passed the initial screening, then a plant visit was scheduled. Prospective employees who were

about to receive their doctoral degrees, were required to make a presentation on their thesis topic before representatives of all departments who might have expressed an interest in considering the candidate for employment. If all the departments were in New

Jersey, then their representatives would gather in one location for the thesis review. If departments were in different states, then the candidate would travel to the different sites to repeat this presentation. In my case, I was required to present in Holmdel, New Jersey and in Andover, Massachusetts, called Merrimac Valley [MV] in company lexicon.

There was a special express bus that left New York City's Port Authority Terminal at 7:00 AM and arrived at the Holmdel location about ten minutes before the starting time of the work day. I had to take the subway from the upper West Side to the terminal in good time to catch the bus since I was not a regular rider. After signing in at the Labs front desk, I was escorted by my host to the conference room to make my presentation. After presenting a paper at a conference in Monterey, California in November 1968, and defending my thesis in April 1969, I was pretty adept at describing my work by this time, which was in May, 1969. Afterwards, I left the room to allow the department to confer on who was still interested in further interviews with me. I spent the rest of the morning interviewing with the first department, then had lunch in the company cafeteria where i spoke with a few Columbia graduates who had joined a year or two earlier. Then I went around with two other departments until closing time after 5:00PM. A group of those who had talked with me took me to a restaurant for dinner and I was put on a regular Port Authority bus to New York. By the time I got to New York after 9:00 PM, I was totally exhausted.

Then I was expected to fly to Massachusetts the next morning or two to repeat the whole process with other departments at Merrimac Valley. But before I left Holmdel, I had been asked to rank the departments in my order of preference, and if my first or second choice had expressed an interest in hiring me, then we would have a match. So I asked my recruiter whether I had such a match at Holmdel. He said there was and I then asked if I could forego the trip to MV. Apparently, this was quite an unusual request, but he agreed to it and promised to start the paperwork to get me an offer, which he did. One of those expecting me at MV, Ming L. Liou was a good friend of my advisor and was looking forward to my visit. He was disappointed at my truncation of the process and for several years after I had joined the company, he reminded me of the fact whenever we met. Another reason that I wanted to take a position in New Jersey was that I still had some revisions to make on my thesis and submit the required number of copies to the dean's office. I could commute to Holmdel while living in New York using the special bus that I rode to the interview. I was able to start in July 1969, and continued to commute to New Jersey from New York for almost ten months before relocating to New Jersey. It was an interesting experience going out of New York City to work while ninety percent of others were coming into New York City, coping with long traffic lines at the Lincoln and Holland Tunnel toll booths every day. I have since tried to avoid such common traffic patterns throughout my working life by choosing where we lived in relation to where I worked.

My first department was called the Electronic Telephone Department. Their main project was the design of a new telephone station set in which many of the key functions were implemented by solid state devices such as diodes, transistors and integrated circuit operational amplifiers. By replacing inductors and transformers, the unit was so light that extra weights were added to the handset and base to keep them some stability. When the solid state revolution was launched with the invention of the transistor, the areas that first benefited were switching and long distance transmission systems. By mid 1960s, the costs of solid state devices had come down enough for us to consider using them in customer equipment. The logic was simple. A piece of central office equipment costing $100,000 was shared by 10,000 customers, so the cost per customer was $10. On the other hand, a piece of equipment costing $100 dedicated to one customer had to be paid for by that one customer. So those designing customer station devices had a different economic constraint than those designing switching and toll transmission systems.

As it turned out, once the laboratory design and development were completed, the economic considerations began to weigh in. The management people asked the technical people what would happen to the millions of basic 500 set telephones if the electronic telephone was so attractive that every customer would want one in place of their old sets. Since all the phones were leased to the customers, the telephone operating companies would be saddled with millions of obsolete equipment. While I was not personally involved with these financial and marketing arguments, we were made to understand that the electronic telephone was dead on arrival. As a new employee, it was a valuable lesson: we could invent anything we cared to do, but whether it will see the light of day and actually serve people was an entirely different matter.

The demise of the electronic telephone project turned out to be a blessing in disguise for my professional career. While I was on that project, my assignment was to improve upon the electronic hybrid circuit, which interfaces the four wires from the microphone and speaker in the handset to the two wires going to the central office. But after the termination of the electronic telephone project, I was assigned to an exploratory projects group, where we were charged with developing new uses of the telephone network besides speech. Data transmission and reception were already major responsibilities in other departments. However, our group sought to provide end-to-end signaling in common household telephone sets by building in Touchtone and other data receivers. During this phase, from 1971 to 1973, I received patents for voice recognition circuits and integrated circuit multi-frequency receivers.

In pursuing this objective, we came up with telephone controls for handicapped users, flat surface dialers, and motion tracking for remote black boards. The most successful output was a point-of sale transaction telephone for automatic credit checking and approval. My assignment on the specific design of this product lasted from 1973 to 1976. Hundreds of these were installed in trial service in Chicago and Columbus, Ohio and this was the only product I worked on in Holmdel that I saw in service at stores. Years later, it is rewarding to see products that we had dreamed of become common household items. Specifically, caller identification devices were frowned upon because the company could only charge for answered calls. Voice mail was also put on a slow pace and only became common after the break-up of the Bell System. In other cases, the advances in technology were even more rapid and revolutionary than we could have foreseen.

As I described earlier, two other areas of the communication system were switching and transmission. By not going to Massachusetts, in 1969, I missed out on exploring the transmission area. But in 1976, a group dealing with the switching of operated assisted calls was being transferred from Holmdel to another Bell Labs location in Naperville, Illinois, called Indian Hill. For almost fifteen years of being in the US, I had only lived in New Jersey and New York, New York. I thought that since the family was still young, we could easily relocate to another state and see some more of the United States. So I volunteered to take the place of one of those who did not wish to relocate, and we moved to Naperville in June 1976.

In the course of this relocation, we enjoyed the generous benefits of working for an arm of the Bell System. The company bought our house in Keyport, New Jersey, paying the average of three appraisals. Also, in lieu of paying for shipping one of our cars, a Chevy Nova, they bought it from us at the bluebook value. So we packed the family into the full-size Ford LTD and drove to Illinois. For safety, we were required to drive only three hundred miles a day. So we stopped overnight in Youngstown, Ohio for the first night, and in Hammond, Indiana for the second night. Then we stayed at a Stouffer's Hotel in Oak Park, Illinois for about three nights while waiting for delivery of our household furniture. When it was all over, they calculated the value of the benefits as income and paid us the estimated tax on the extra income. We were able to settle down comfortably and began the adventure of knowing a different face of the United States.

One of our lasting memories of this period was the severity of the winters as compared to what we had experienced in New Jersey and New York City. Our first winter in 1976 was one of the coldest on record and the next winter in 1977 had record snow fall. In fact, to show that we were not the only tropical birds caught out of place, the inability to remove snow from the streets in a timely manner led to changes in the mayoral election in Chicago in the following year.

At the work place, the experience was also different. As a central office equipment, it was large and about sixty engineers and support staff were involved in continuing engineering and scheduled improvements. Operator services brought out two tendencies of the Bell System. In the early days, every call, local or long distance had to be completed by an operator. As telephone service grew, it was projected that at some point in the future, every high school graduate had to be employed as an operator in order to handle the traffic demand. But long before that point, the switching function was largely automated and the need for operators was reduced to manageable levels. Only special calls such as coin and collect calls required an operator to complete. But as automation was good for the direct-dialed calls, it was also good for operator assisted calls. So a new system called the Traffic Service Position System, TSPS, was developed and installed. It was then improved with new features at regular intervals. When I joined, they had just added the coin detection feature, which greatly reduced the amount of time an operator needed to complete such calls. As was known from the analysis of service or queuing systems, reducing the service times also reduced the number of servers needed to handle a given level of traffic [Erlang Loss and Delay Formulas]. While this made a lot of sense to the engineers and managers, the unions did not take kindly to the loss of membership. One of the next steps was to measure the performance of each individual operator in the time taken to handle each type of call as compared to group averages; the unions did not like this step and made an issue of it in their contract negotiations.

While automation was certainly good and necessary, the regulatory process led to a tendency to overdo it. This was because, as a monopoly, the Bell System was allowed to earn a certain rate of return on its investment. So the large installation of transmission cables and switching machines, depreciated over a forty year period, helped to increase the value of installed capital and hence the amount of money that the company was able to charge for its services. Even the telephones in homes and offices were leased and remained part of the capital base. As its adversaries pointed out, this also led to a delay in replacing obsolete equipment. The constant arguments and court challenges eventually resulted in the breakup of the Bell System in the early 1980s.

In retrospect, I consider it a privilege that a poor village boy would come to the United States from the Niger Delta and become associated with three icons of the society such as Princeton University, Columbia University, and Bell Telephone Laboratories. One of my best friends for over fifty years, Dr. O.O. Omatete enjoyed a similar experience by receiving degrees from Princeton

University, the University of California at Berkeley, and then working at the Oak Ridge National Laboratories for over a decade. We were so lucky.

Those years at Bell Labs were the most productive of my professional life. In addition to the physical and technical resources, the people around you were very inspiring. The record of innovation from the very beginning of the Labs was on display everywhere. When one is surrounded by so many smart people, it tends to rub off on you. During my teaching days, I used to state when and where I met some of the pioneers of our profession that we were reading about in our textbooks, such as Sydney Darlington or Robert Lucky. Those people did their pioneering works in the 1940s and 1950s, but were still active in the 1960s and 1970s while I was at the Labs. The students I was teaching in the 1990s were born in the 1970s, so my innocent historical comments made me appear ancient to them. I quickly learned not to make those comments.

5: LUNCHEON AT COLUMBIA FACULTY CLUB, 1970

CHAPTER FIVE

Columbia University: 1965-1969

As I started my senior year at Princeton University in fall 1964, I decided that I would go to graduate school because I thought that I had a lot more to learn about my chosen field of electrical engineering and the special area of communication systems. I had taken one senior course in the area of statistical communication theory, preceded by junior courses in electronics, microwaves and electromagnetism. Reading the textbooks and references, I knew that my undergraduate education had just scratched the surface of the available body of knowledge in these areas. Besides these were, and continue to be, part of a rapidly advancing field, and it would take a lifetime of continuing education to keep up.

I applied to take the graduate record examination which graduate schools used for admission decisions. I also wrote to many universities for their graduate school catalogs and application forms for admission and financial aid. This time I was much better informed, unlike the time when I applied for admission to

Princeton University from Nigeria. After three years at Princeton, and having come from a high school in a small provincial town of Ughelli in the Niger Delta, I wanted to experience a large metropolitan environment to expand my horizon. We had come through New York City when we came to the US in 1962 and for each summer and Christmas break, I had spent some time in New York. So studying in New York City was an attractive possibility for me and Columbia University became my first choice for graduate study.

In submitting my application for admission to Columbia, I did not know how competitive I would be against other applicants. My graduate record scores in quantitative aptitude and engineering were good, but the verbal score was just average. So I applied to three other schools:

Stevens Institute of Technology, Hoboken, New Jersey; University of Illinois, Urbana-Champaign; and the University of Michigan, Ann Arbor. Once I received a letter of admission from Columbia, my mind was immediately made up.

In April 1965, I had received a letter from the Nigerian Consulate, announcing that all Nigerian students specializing in science and engineering fields would be awarded a scholarship for graduate study up to the master's level. So about two weeks before formal graduation ceremonies at Princeton, I enrolled for summer school at Columbia. I registered for a French reading course because I would be required to demonstrate the ability to read technical journals in a foreign language later in my doctoral studies. I also enrolled in an applied mathematics course dealing with complex variables and matrices, and a course in atomic physics. I had taken undergraduate courses in the mathematics and physics areas, so what I really wanted was to take a course in chemistry, which I had not studied since higher school certificate at Ughelli. However, my friend Dr. Henry Bozimo, who was in graduate school in the chemistry department in Columbia at the time, strongly discouraged me. His reason was that I would do badly and give us a bad name after he had spent two years creating a good reputation for us Africans. In hindsight, he might have been right because I was not used to the rapid pace of summer school and barely passed the physics course, although I had an 'A' in the mathematics course. This was the first time and last that I ever took a summer course for credit in all my school days.

Later, I used the six credits from the physics and mathematics courses to qualify for the Master's degree in Electrical Engineering in May 1966. I needed these six credit hours because starting from the fall, I also had a teaching assistantship from the electrical engineering department as my financial aid package. I was limited to only twelve credit hours a semester and therefore earned only twenty-four credit hours from the fall and spring semesters.

Receiving the master's degree was very helpful because it allowed me to declare a goal of studying for the doctoral degree. It also enabled me to convert from a student visa to a permanent resident visa, using the existing laws. First, after the Soviet launch of the Sputnik earth orbiting satellite in 1957, the US had passed laws encouraging the immigration of scientists and engineers. Also, in 1967, the Biafran Civil War was in full swing in the Niger Delta, and being a non-Igbo, I had become a refugee for the brief period that the Igbos had occupied all of the Niger Delta. So as an engineer and a refugee from a war zone, I received my permanent resident visa with minimum effort. In later decades, as the immigration laws became more restrictive and I witnessed Cubans and Haitians dying in their attempts to migrate to the US, I could not help but wonder how my destiny had placed me at the right place at the right time.

From that summer on and for the next four years, New York City became part of my growing up experience, and the Big Apple did not disappoint. I became one of those millions of immigrants who have started their new lives in America by passing through New York City. Even though most people eventually moved on to other cities, there were always enough diversity in the city to make anyone feel welcome. In fact, there was a commercial running in those days that celebrated this diversity. It stated that there were more Jamaicans in New York than in Kingston, Jamaica; another was that there were more people of African descent in New York than in Accra, Ghana or that there were more Irish in New York than in Dublin, Ireland. I have forgotten the product that was being advertised, but I can clearly remember the content of the commercial because of the welcoming effect it had on me. The lessons I learned from the streets of New York City have been just as valuable to me for the last forty years as the lessons I learned in the classrooms of Columbia University. Of course, I was not the first to learn this lesson. The founders of Columbia University knew this when they insisted in naming the school "Columbia University In The City of New York".

My daughter has been living in New York City for the last ten years, pursuing undergraduate and graduate studies at New York University. I have therefore had reasons to visit New York once or twice a year in that period. I have seen how the city has changed from decade to decade. When I first arrived in 1965, the city was apparently not in the best of shape. They had a mayor, Robert Wagner, who had been in office for a long time. When he ran for re-election in 1966 against John Lindsey, one of the commercials for the Lindsey campaign stated that Mr. Lindsey was fresh and everyone else was tired. This seemed to have worked and Mr. Lindsey was elected mayor. I had no idea what the crime rate or other quality of life issues were like at that time, since I was totally focused on my studies. I also missed out on a lot of fun apparently, as some of the other students at the time told me decades later that they conspired not to let me know of some parties because they thought I would disapprove of some activities, probably related to drugs and alcohol. The mid to late 1960s were generally a turbulent period in the USA. There were the anti-Vietnam War movement, the civil rights movement and the hippie rebellious lifestyles. One of the phenomena that I remember was the large amount of psychedelic "LSD-inspired" abstract graffiti on the subway trains. Apparently, these were spray-painted on the trains during their overnight stops at the terminals, and the clean-up crews were overwhelmed and just let them stay. To a visitor or newcomer, they looked disorderly and perhaps falsely indicated that the authorities did not care. Now when I visit, the state of the subway trains is one of the things I marvel at, but it must have come at a high price. In the four years that I lived in the city, the fare for subway rides went from fifteen cents to twenty-five cents. Now it is over two dollars.

One of the ways that I used to cope with homesickness was to visit Harlem regularly. Typically on Friday afternoons or Saturday mornings, when I wanted to take time off from my studies, I would hike down a footpath through Morningside Park to 125th Street in Harlem for a haircut and just strolling along the street between 8th Avenue and Lexington Avenue. In those days, this area was full of black businesses and street vendors. But I found most comforting was to observe the faces of the black people. Almost always, I would see people that reminded me of people I had known back at home and somehow that made me less homesick, and I was ready to go back to Morningside Heights for another week of battling with my academic adversaries.

Another source of learning outside the classroom was the New York Times. In particular, every Sunday, I would spend two or more hours reading the magazine, book review and editorial sections. Also, the reporting on international affairs was comprehensive and included fair coverage of African events. During the Biafran civil war in Nigeria, the Times was a source of objective information as both sides of the war tried to use the media for propaganda purposes and put out inaccurate information to gain sympathy and support.

After receiving the master's degree in June, 1966, I started my doctoral studies in earnest in September. The first objective was to earn another thirty graduate credit hours. Again in each of the fall 1966 and the spring 1967 semesters, I served as a teaching assistant and was restricted to enrolling for twelve credits per semester. I used these two semesters taking all the lecture classes in communication systems, circuits and network theory, electronics and electromagnetic theory. This exhausted the knowledge in textbooks, and we were then left to keep up with the newest knowledge through seminars, reading refereed journals, and communicating with other graduate students and professors on the research they were carrying out that had not yet been published. This was very important because between the time an article was submitted and published in a refereed journal or conference record, it could take up to nine months or a year and half. In some cases where our professors were editors of some of these journals, we were able to read the articles as they were submitted and helped our professors to make the decision to accept for publication or not.

In summer 1966, I had worked at a research laboratory run by some faculty and research associates on contracts with the Advanced Research Projects Agency, a predecessor of the Defense Advanced Research Projects Agency [DARPA]. But in summer 1967, I took time off to prepare for the next milestone in my doctoral studies. This was the doctoral qualifying examination. It was an eight hour examination; four hours in the morning on fundamentals of the undergraduate curriculum and four hours in the afternoon on four selected areas of the graduate curriculum. In the two years of being a teaching assistant, I had been grading student homework papers and some test papers for the undergraduate courses. So we had worked closely with the professors and this became an advantage over the students who were on fellowships and the students who were already working full time in industry. Even with this edge, I was very unhappy with my performance after the exam because I thought I had not done my best. However, after about two weeks, the results were posted and I was one of ten who had passed out of about thirty who had taken the exam.

As of fall 1967, I was accepted as a research assistant under Professor Henry Meadows, under a grant funded by the National Aeronautical and Space Administration [NASA] and this lasted for the bulk of the next two years, except for one semester in which I was funded by a National Science Foundation [NSF] grant. That is why my doctoral thesis was submitted to NASA as a technical report and has been archived in the database of national technical reports.

In the fall 1967 and spring 1968 semesters, I took doctoral seminar courses in electrical engineering and took twelve credits of applied mathematics courses as a minor area. This knowledge of mathematics played a significant role in the doctoral thesis that I eventually generated, but also throughout my professional career, particularly the two decades of university teaching.

During the spring 1968 semester, after the assassination of the Reverend Dr. Martin Luther King, Jr. in April 1968, there were riots on the campus, with the University's acquisition of land inside Morningside Park for an indoor athletic facility as an additional grievance. The university was closed for several weeks, and at the end of the disturbance, we were given the option of either taking formal end of semester examinations for regular letter grades, or to accept Pass/Fail grades based on work done before the disturbances. Since it was the last semester that I would take normal classes, and since the affected classes were the applied mathematics courses for my minor, I decided to take the standard examinations and received "A" grades in the two courses.

After passing the qualifying exam and completing the thirty credit hours, the only remaining obstacle to receiving a doctoral degree was to complete a doctoral thesis, defend it before a panel of professors from my department, including my advisor, and representatives of other departments in the School of Engineering and Applied Science [SEAS] one of whom had taught me in one of my applied mathematics courses. At Columbia, we could choose to receive a Doctor of Engineering degree administered by SEAS, or a Doctor of Philosophy [Ph.D.] administered by the Graduate Faculties for all the departments in the Humanities, Arts and Sciences. The only difference was that SEAS required reading proficiency in only one foreign language; I chose the Doctor of Engineering degree and satisfied the foreign language requirement by translating two pages of a French article in Wireless and Cable journal.

The main requirement of the doctoral thesis has always been to make a contribution of knowledge in a chosen field. In electrical engineering in 1967 and 1968, the cutting edge of technology was the capability to manufacture discrete solid state devices such as transistors and diodes for signal processing, and silicon controlled rectifiers [SCR] at for power processing. Also, small scale and medium scale integrated digital circuits, [SSI, MSI] were becoming available for high value products such as military and space applications. This was the state of the art of the day.

The key characteristic of semiconductor devices that

we had to study in the universities was that they could implement circuits with resistors and capacitors, but not inductors which required coils of insulated wire wound around a magnetic core. Therefore, there were a number of doctoral theses dealing with circuits with resistors and capacitors [RC] or RC circuits with an active component such as an operational amplifier, Active-RC circuits. The Department of Electrical Engineering at Columbia University was quite productive as a Ph.D. factory, graduating three to five doctoral students a year. As a teaching or research assistant, I had shared office space with several of these graduates, and was therefore familiar with the routine.

I studied several of the theses of my former colleagues at Columbia, as well as one from Stanford University. Naturally there was a wide range in the quality of innovation, effort and creativity among the theses accepted as meeting the requirements. Some were as low as seventy pages while others were over two hundred pages, even though we could say a lot in a few pages using mathematical equations. I tried to strike a happy medium and ended up with a thesis of one hundred and twenty pages.

One thesis studied the properties of circuits using any number of resistors and capacitors and only one inductor. The justification for this was that the resistors and capacitors could be implemented as an integrated circuit, leaving only the inductor as an external component. Another thesis dealt with multiplication of the RC product of an integrated circuit by including a switching element in the circuit. The motivation for this work was that the silicon wafers were limited in size and so the magnitudes of the resistances and capacitances that can be built were limited. By using a switch to interrupt the exponential decay, it produced the effect of larger values of the RC elements. Finally, I got a copy of a thesis by Y. Sun written at Stanford University which obtained the time-domain responses of circuits with resistors, capacitors and periodically operated switches by analyzing the circuit in the open and closed states of the switches and piecing the solutions together over time.

After months of study, I proposed a thesis studying the response of circuits with inductors, capacitors and switches [SLC] which were operated in such a way that there was no loss of power if all elements were assumed to be ideal. The lossless constraint limited the location of the switches with respect to the inductors and capacitors so that there would be no interruption of inductor currents or shorting of capacitor voltages as a result of switching action; interrupting inductor currents or shorting capacitor voltages would create a spark or flash which represents a conversion of electrical power into light or heat and hence a loss of power from the electrical state. This then allowed continuity of those quantities at all switching instants and hence continuity in piecing solutions across switching states. The lossless property contributes to efficiency in power processing which was very important to NASA. In 1968, the public attention of the space program was on the Apollo moon landing mission, which was eventually accomplished in July 1969. But in 1968, engineers were looking ahead to the permanent space stations which relied on solar panels for electrical power. The output of the solar panels was direct current electricity, which had to be processed to other standard dc voltages to power electronic circuits, and to standard alternating current electricity to power motors and other machinery on board the station.

The title of my thesis was "Periodically Switched Lossless Networks". Instead of just time domain responses as Dr. Sun had derived for switched RC circuits, I was able to derive frequency-domain network functions for the SLC circuits. The mathematics courses I had taken for my minor had provided me with knowledge of integral transforms, discrete-time systems, differential and difference equations, functions of a matrix and complex variables. This background knowledge not only enabled me to formulate and solve the resulting differential and difference equations, but also to interpret the results and suggest potential applications. In summary, the circuit was defined by a system of first-order differential equations during the rest intervals of the switches. The solution of these equations included an initial state vector at the switching instants. Equating the final value from one interval to the initial value of the following interval resulted in a first-order difference equation for the initial values. The solution of this difference equation depended on only one global initial value which was used to identify transient and steady-state solutions of the system of equations. The steady-state forced response to a complex exponential driving function then defined the transfer function of the circuit.

I have wondered why NASA archived my thesis in a national database after nearly forty years. Did the storage technology just made it easier, or had they found it useful? Was it seen as a standard doctoral thesis or was it a model product?

After the summer of 1968, I was able to submit my first technical paper for presentation at the Asilomar Conference on Circuits and Systems in Monterey, California. When I returned from this presentation in November, 1968, my advisor was quite pleased with the feedback he had received from some of his professor friends who had heard my presentation. So then I knew I had done something worthy of a doctoral degree, and spent the rest of the winter and spring writing and revising the thesis.

In 1969, the theses were typed on carbon paper and copies run off on a press; it was slow and difficult to make changes. I was able to defend the thesis in April, also called an oral examination. When this had been judged satisfactory, I made some more changes, wrote another conference paper and got a letter from the department stating that I had met all requirements for the Doctor of Engineering degree. I then went to work at Bell Telephone Laboratories, starting on July 14, 1969. I took some time copying and binding a number of copies of my thesis for the department, the dean's office and for NASA, the sponsor of the research grant that supported me for two years. These were deposited at the appropriate offices in September 1969, which became the official date for my degree.

6: RECREATIONAL SOCCER TEAM, PRINCETON, 1964

CHAPTER SIX

Princeton University: 1962-1965

I first heard of Princeton University in 1960 when my friend Henry Bozimo was admitted there. Henry had served as an advance scout for me before when he went from primary school in Bomadi to Government College, Ughelli two years ahead of me. The following year, 1961, three of the top students from Ughelli [O.O. Omatete, Victor Diejomaoh and Michael Edo] also went to Princeton. Going to Princeton then became a personal goal for me also, even though I had not quite understood what it would take to get there. But the events that made it possible were already in motion.

Nigeria became an independent country in 1960, after fifty years of being a colony in the British Empire. In the height of the Cold War pitting The United States and its capitalist allies in Western Europe against the Soviet Union and its communist allies in Eastern Europe, the new African nations that were gaining independence from European colonization became centers of competition for influence by the opposing blocks. One of the ways that were devised by both sides was to offer scholarships to young people to study in the US and in all the countries of the Soviet block. The justification for this was that the new countries needed highly trained professionals and bureaucrats to manage their affairs in the community of nations. This was quite valid, especially for some of the other countries such the Belgian Congo which was extremely short of university-trained personnel. But we were also aware of the hidden agenda of both parties to influence and gain the loyalty of the future leaders of these countries. We always considered the possibility that some of those program assistants who were friendly to us might be agents of the Central Intelligence Agency reporting on our political attitudes to their bosses. Most of us never expected to be political leaders, so it never bothered us that we were being monitored. If they were actually spying on us, I suppose that they had their money's worth on account of those few who eventually became senators, governors, cabinet ministers and even presidential candidates. Of course all this was of little consequence after the demise of the Soviet Union in the 1990s.

Nigeria already had four universities at independence, and Nigerians had been training in Britain for generations, so our situation was not so dire as in many other places. However, by the fact of containing one quarter of the population of Sub-Saharan Africa, any program had to give a lion's share to Nigeria.

The particular program that brought us to the US was called the African Scholarship Program of American Universities [ASPAU]. It was created as a joint venture in which the home countries paid for our transportation to and from the US; the living expenses were paid by the

United States Agency for International Development, USAID. The American universities contributed full scholarships for tuition, room and board. The program started small with tens of students in 1960 and expanded to hundreds by the third wave which included me in 1962. The program continued throughout the 1960s before being phased out and had served thousands from many countries in that decade.

The selection process started with an application listing our high school graduation credentials. Then we were called to Lagos to take the SAT verbal, quantitative and selected achievement examinations. Finally, each student was interviewed by a panel of Nigerians and Americans to select final winners. Of course, things did not proceed so smoothly. For me, the telegram calling me to Lagos arrived after the date of the tests. I was then teaching mathematics and Latin at the Saint Brendan's Catholic secondary school in Bomadi, so the telegram was received in Warri and then carried by boat to Bomadi. Luckily, I was able to report to Lagos about a week later, and took the written tests. Apparently, I was not the only person from remote corners of the country who had been affected by the limitations of our posts and telegraph infrastructure. It was a big relief because I thought I had missed my opportunity to come to the US and had been quite distraught

During the personal interview, I was asked what books I had read lately. From the library at Saint Brendan's, I had read many western novels, but what came to mind was a more contemporary novel, "The Last Angry Man" about a Jewish storekeeper hassled by street gangs in Brooklyn, and talked about many social problems of the

1950s in the USA. In the course of the discussion, I said that I expected that many of those social problems had been solved a decade later. This brought out a lot of laughter from the Americans on the panel, since they thought that I was either very optimistic or very naive. It was much later that I learned some of the reactions of the people to my interview, during the summer of 1963 or 1964, from one of the program administrative assistants in New York City.

The application form had also asked what three American universities I would like to attend if selected, in order of preference, and my response had been Princeton, Princeton, Princeton!! At the interview, I was asked to explain this arrogance, so I mentioned the four people from my high school who were attending Princeton and that it would help me settle down quickly and attend to my studies. One of them, either Bozimo or Omatete, had sent me Princeton's undergraduate catalog, with a picture of Nassau Hall on the cover, and I was quite fascinated by it. I had grown up in the watery section of the Niger Delta. There the land is unstable and houses did not last up to fifty years, with the thatch and mud construction materials contributing to early collapse. I appreciated buildings that were hundreds of years old such as Westminster Abbey that we had seen in pictures during the colonial era. Again, I was not particularly aware of the iconic status of Princeton University, but the panel was quite sympathetic, apparently because they knew that I was one of the star candidates, as I learned later.

During high school, we had become fairly familiar with the more famous British Universities. Some of our teachers, both British and Nigerian, had attended those universities. Also, the University of Ibadan had started as a College of the University of London. Cambridge University was the leader of the syndicate overseeing our secondary school leaving examinations and all our certificates bore their logo. We were all aware of the competition for preeminence between Oxford and Cambridge. But when it came to American universities, those of us from the provincial towns were quite clueless. Those from cities like Lagos, which had a library operated by the United States Information Service, were able to read various university catalogs and were better informed. There was also considerable confusion about the use of the term "College" as part of a university. When we got to talking and some one mentioned that they were heading to Harvard College or Columbia College, we were not quite sure how they were related to Harvard University or Columbia University. Looking back, I feel we should have known better, since the University of Ibadan was originally a College of the University of London, as I said above. Our confusion was really not being clear about the difference between graduate and undergraduate university education.

Also, we used the term "college" for our secondary grammar schools which ran college preparatory programs of study. I know I was not the only one confused by these terms at the time because some of those who were admitted to some well known US colleges such as Marist or Haverford were concerned that they would be required to repeat part of their high school curriculum. They thought this would cause them to fall behind their classmates and affect their seniority in the civil service when they returned to Nigeria. In the end, so much of our fears were unfounded for many reasons. First, by 1962, the US colleges were familiar with the quality of secondary education in Nigeria at that time and all those who had received the Higher School Certificate were given advanced placement and started as sophomores. They were thus exempted from the usual freshmen courses in composition, physical education, US History, et cetera. This was my own experience at Princeton, so that I was admitted with the class of 1966 and graduated with the class of 1965, a fact that still creates problems for the alumni records department. A few of the other colleges were less flexible, and some of the students were forced to seek transfers to other schools.

When I finally got my letter of admission in May, 1962, I had a busy time trying to get ready to leave for the US early in August. As soon as the term ended at St. Brendan's, I resigned and left to stay with relatives in Lagos while taking care of the passport and visa requirements. Lagos was the federal capital then and the US Embassy was situated there. So all the selected students came together to receive some preliminary orientation and get our travel documents. We did some things together as a group, such as our visit to the health department for chest X-rays and vaccinations for the contagious diseases of the time. We also had to get endorsements from our political representatives and highly placed civil servants in the police or armed forces for our passport and visa requirements. This was the occasion for my introduction to Melford Okilo, who was then Parliamentary Secretary for one of the federal ministries and a member of the House of Parliament. He was later governor of Rivers State from 1979-1983.

One of the questions that I got tired of answering was "How did you get into Princeton?" My friend Omatete also had the same experience. The follow up questions were: Was your father a king or big chief in your country? Was your father a Prime Minister or President in your country? We actually had a son of the President of Togo, and sons of cabinet ministers from the Ivory Coast and Malawi in my Princeton class and they both became cabinet ministers in their countries. Was your father an oil billionaire? Alas, those had not yet been created in Nigeria in 1962. Our answers to all these questions were NO, NO, and NO. We said we were just very lucky guys from the Niger Delta, which did not satisfy our interrogators. They had exhausted all their stereotypes of Princeton students of those days, royals, high government ties and great wealth. Even though Princeton's admission policies have been liberalized significantly in favor of diversity, still the admission ratio is like one thousand admitted out of twelve thousand excellent applicants. In 1962, Princeton was still an all-male school and we did not have a female counterpart like Harvard and Wellesley or Columbia and Barnard. Princeton became co-educational in the 1970s and the competition for admission is still as fierce as ever.

Even though luck played a role, we were admitted on merit as well. Dr. Omatete later reviewed the records of the ASPAU program in their office in New York, and found that I had scored the highest in the SAT exams out of all the students from Nigeria. Further, in the previous year, one of the Ughelli students had also scored the highest, so the program administrators were left wondering how an unknown school from the Niger Delta could have produced such a result. In the higher school certificate examinations in 1961, I took five subjects: Applied Mathematics, Pure Mathematics, Physics, Chemistry and General Paper [an English composition and comprehension test]. On a scale of 1 to 9 on each subject, I had scored 1, 1, 2, 2, and 3. This was not only the best that year, but was also best in the sciences ever in our school's history. Diejomaoh had scored

three ones in social study and humanity subjects the previous year. Soon after independence, the quality of

science education, particularly the laboratories, had declined significantly, such that one of my young cousins who attended Ughelli in the 1970s said that my record was still unbroken and might stand forever.

Some Nigerian tribes teach their children to tout their own achievements because they say that if you do not blow your own horn, no one will blow it for you. My tribe is not one of those, so we never talk about our own achievements or those of our children. So as an Izon man, I found it very difficult to explain how I had gotten to Princeton, and in fact, many Princeton students and alumni act the same way. I have not actually found out what I scored in the SATs. I assume that they will be on my Princeton transcript, but I had not needed my Princeton transcript since completing my graduate applications and have never kept a copy for my self.

The physical journey to Princeton was also quite fascinating. We started out from Nigeria on August 2, 1962, about six weeks before the start of classes. First we flew to Paris on an Air Afrique charter flight for the ninety plus Nigerian group. It was my first air trip. We stopped for refueling in Niamey, Niger, before proceeding to

Paris. After about two days of sightseeing in Paris, we took a train to the port of Cherbourg. We then boarded a ship, the S.S. Groote Beer, Dutch for The Great Bear operated by Holland-America Lines. We then crossed the English Channel to South Hampton, England, sailing past the cliffs of Dover. Here we picked up a group of American students who had gone to spend some portion of the summer in England. Some of them had also been hired to lead an orientation program for us as we sailed across the Atlantic Ocean. Somehow, one of the students leading us in the orientation was my friend Henry Bozimo, who had by then completed two years at Princeton. I got a few extra lessons about Princeton from him in addition to the general program.

By the time we got on the ship, students from other African countries had joined us. In the first year in 1960, the program only included Nigerians and Congolese. In 1962, we had students from Ethiopia, Sierra Leone, Liberia, Malawi, Madagascar, Tanganyika and Zanzibar, which were then separate countries before becoming the joint country of Tanzania a few years later. These were the independent countries in Sub-Saharan, non-Arabic speaking Africa. If there were students from Ghana, which had achieved independence in 1957, I do not recall meeting any of them. There were also French-speaking students, but they were heading first to intensive English Language institute, so I did not interact with them during the trip. The Nigerian contingent of ninety-four was the most from any country and therefore we were most visible everywhere. There were also African-American students among the instructors, and I am sure they were just as confused about us as we were about them. In fact, even though I did not get close enough to any of them to get first hand information, it was rumored among the Africans that some of the African-Americans were not happy that we were heading to universities like Princeton, Harvard and Yale which had none or only a few African-American students. Apparently, those who hired them to give us orientation had not totally oriented them. In fact, my Princeton class had one African-American besides the four Africans on the ASPAU program.

For most of the orientation program, we were divided into groups according to the region of the US that we were going to study in. I was in the Mid-Atlantic coast group for those going to New York, New Jersey and Pennsylvania. There were groups for those going to South-Atlantic coast [Maryland, Washington D.C. and Virginia], the South [

Georgia, the Carolinas and Tennessee], New England, Mid-West, the Plain States and the Pacific Coast. I do not recall anything in particular that they taught us during the week. First, I knew that I had my own four-person orientation team at Princeton, so whatever I might have missed would be filled in later. Then the trip was quite rough, as the ship was not particularly big and many of us suffered from sea-sickness half of the time. Even for those of us from the Niger Delta who had been close to the ocean, this was our first ocean going journey and many of us had not been back since. I think as part of our feedback, we advised them to fly us directly to some solid ground and conduct the orientation program there. I do not recall whether or not they took our advice.

It was a big relief when we first sighted the coast of the US off Maine. We were also quite excited at all the adventures that surely awaited us in this new land. We sailed down the coast, eventually entering New York harbor, past the Statue of Liberty and stopped at a berth in Hoboken, New Jersey. As we came down the coast, immigration officials boarded the ship and processed our visa documents. So right after we landed, most of the students were taken by bus to the Henry Hudson Hotel in mid-Manhattan to await transportation to their respective destinations.

Another of the programs that had been arranged for us was called The Experiment in International Living. We had come a few weeks before classes so that we could spend time with American families before proceeding to our campuses. My Experiment family consisted of a father who was the United Nations correspondent for the then "Chicago News" newspaper. The mother was a stay-at-home mom which was the norm in those days. They had four children, two girls ages nine and seven, and two boys ages five and three. They lived in Englewood, New Jersey. They picked me up as soon as I was done at Hoboken, and thus started a relation that lasted until the mother died in 1999. She was proud of me and shared the joys of my accomplishments and sympathized at my disappointments. She was particularly proud when I graduated with Honors in 1965. When I was asked how I had entered Princeton, she always answered that I was very smart, and my graduation sort of confirmed it for her.

From memory and through pictures, I can recall the additional introduction to life in the USA that they provided. I had visits to the Statue of Liberty and the Bronx Zoo. I also attended several parties and receptions at UN headquarters and legations of the various countries.

I met many of the world leaders of the day, including the then Secretary-General, U Thant of Burma. I also met Indira Gandhi, Charles De Gaulle of France , and Konrad Adenauer of West Germany. I met and spent time on many occasions with Adlai Stephenson, Princeton Class of 1922, the US Ambassador to the United Nations under President Kennedy and two-time presidential candidate against Dwight Eisenhower. He was a regular visitor to the family and took particular interest in me as I was about to embark on my Princeton education.

Finally the day came for me to report to Princeton. There was a week of freshman orientation and other events, although I was starting as a sophomore. I was housed in Holder Hall which was a typical sophomore dormitory. I had three other room-mates from Maryland, New York and Vermont. The first task was to register for appropriate classes. When we left Nigeria, the newspaper report had listed my area of study as Telecommunications. While in high school during the campaign for independence, we had bought into the rhetoric of the politicians that we needed engineers and scientists to develop our countries economically. Therefore the sciences, engineering and economics were the most popular choices for college majors among the African student groups. Since I was from the riverine area of Nigeria, I had considered studying marine engineering. However, being also from a remote area, I was fascinated by the possibilities of communication with remote areas by radio. So I settled on studying telecommunications and thus landed in the electrical engineering department as the closest to my career interests. It has been a life long love ever since.

As I have stated earlier, I have been twice traumatized

by the fact of living in remote and isolated places. The first was being scared out of my wits by a total eclipse of the sun in the 1940s, an event that was a source of anticipation and enjoyment throughout the affected areas, but apparently came as a complete sacrifice to residents of my village. I have wondered why no one in our village had picked up some newspaper or radio report of that impending event. The second was due to not having a telegraph receiving station at Bomadi that delayed my ASPAU invitation by days. If I had not made it on a make-up date, my life could have been significantly different, for better or for worse. With my high school credentials, I could have my pick of any university in Nigeria so that life could still have been comfortable. When I was teaching electromagnetic theory, of fields and action at a distance and propagation of waves through space, I had these thoughts in the back of my mind as I smiled to myself.

Needless to say, that first year was very demanding. I enrolled in sophomore level general engineering courses in statics, strength of materials and thermodynamics. I also took an atomic physics class and a mathematics class on differential equations. I was fairly prepared for my classes except the laboratory portion of the physics course. My high school physics classes had spent too much time on heat, light and sound, and not enough time on electricity, magnetism and atomic physics. So I had to work hard to make up for this deficiency. In the fall semester, I foolishly volunteered to play soccer which was not very popular among the native students, so the team had a good portion of foreign students. I played well enough on the junior varsity team to receive a letter, and was expected to start on the varsity team the following year. However, the academic pressure did not allow me to attend all practice sessions and I had to drop out. In my senior year, I played with an informal team organized by a soccer loving professor of geology originally from Belgium, and we played friendly matches in New York and New Jersey.

The spring semester was much better. At the end of the school year, the ASPAU office published a list of those students who had done well in the classes at their respective colleges and universities. This was part of their public

relations effort to justify and build support for the program with their funding sources. Princeton used a number grading scale from one to seven and my average was like a B plus. I was surprised to find my name on the list. In any event, I was on my way to achieving my academic objective.

7: GCU SCHOOL PREFECTS AND PRINCIPAL, 1961

CHAPTER SEVEN

Government College Ughelli: 1954-1961

As I approached the end of primary education in 1954, the idea of attending secondary school began to form in my mind. Needless to say, not even primary school was compulsory in our remote district, so clearly, secondary education was a rare opportunity for the privileged few or very lucky individuals like me. It took quite a few acts of providence to make it happen.

As I stated earlier, the term "college" was used in Nigeria to describe grammar schools that prepared students for further education in a university. This was probably to distinguish these schools from the vocational and technical schools which prepared students for skilled careers. Soon after my days, there were new schools called "modern schools" for those career oriented students, who could also proceed to Teacher Training Colleges to teach in the primary grades.

Primary education was organized into one infant grade similar to kindergarten, and six grades named

"Standard" One through Standard Six. At the end, after passing an exit examination, one was awarded a Primary School Leaving Certificate. Just before independence, and several times since, there have been different re-organizations of both primary and secondary education to meet various perceived needs of the country, with highly mixed results as far as I can tell.

I transferred to attend the "Native Administration Primary School" in Bomadi in Western Ijaw District of Delta Province in 1953, starting in Standard Four. I had completed Standard Three at a Church Missionary School, CMS, [Anglican] in my own village of Isampou some thirty miles away. For budget reasons, especially for lack of trained Anglican teachers, my village school at that time went only up to Standard Three. Beyond that, we had to transfer to another CMS school in Patani, quite far by boat in those days, or transfer to government run non-religious schools. The nearest NA school was at Aleibri, which was next to Isampou, but I chose to go to Bomadi, three villages away [Aleibri, Tuomo, Anyamasa, Bomadi] because I had relatives there that I could live with while attending school. Even before independence, the term "Native" was changed to "Local" for obvious political reasons and national pride.

It happened that Henry Bozimo had graduated from NA school Bomadi and had been admitted to Government College Ughelli [GCU] in 1952 before I got to Bomadi. This was a big deal and he had become quite a role model for other aspiring students. I first saw him when he came home during breaks in 1953. I do not recall if I was formally introduced to him, but I knew about him. As I said earlier, he became quite an advance scout for me in a fairly remarkable sequence, which stretched from Bomadi to GCU to Princeton to graduate school at Columbia, from where he earned his doctorate in Chemistry.

In 1945, the colonial administrators somehow arrived at the notion that the Niger Delta would be important for the future of Nigeria. They therefore established this government secondary school to train future leaders for the region. It was originally called Warri College, for the nearest significant town in the area. It was later moved to a smaller town of Ughelli where there was plenty of land and renamed Government College, Ughelli.

There were similar secondary schools in other major regions of the country: King's College, Lagos; Government College, Ibadan; Government College, Umuahia; Edo College, Benin City and Government College, Zaria. These served the major ethnic groups in the West, East, Mid-West and Northern regions of the country. Of these, Edo College was the nearest to the western part of the Niger Delta and Government College Umuahia was nearest to the eastern part of the Niger Delta. However, it was clear to the colonial administrators that the small ethnic groups of the Delta were not being adequately served. These included the Urhobos, Isokos and Itsekiris in the West and the not so small ethnic group, the Izons [Ijaws for the colonial civil servants] who were spread along the entire coast of the country almost from Cameroon border to the Dahomey [later called Benin] border. I am native to the central portion of the Izon area, which has bounced between regions in the earlier years after independence and now between states since they were created in 1967 in response to the Biafran civil war.

It was common for the European colonists to confuse the names of people and places. For example, during colonial days, the major ethnic group in Eastern Nigeria were called Ibos, whereas they called themselves Igbos. The British could not pronounce the "gb" sound and simplified it to something they could speak. The Igbos changed their name after independence. Elsewhere, there were similar confusions like Lake Nyasa [Lake lake] in Malawi, Burma for Myanmar and Bombay for Mumbai. All these mistakes are reasonably understandable, but the case of the Izons is hard to figure. The Izons do not have sharp syllables like "j", "ch" or "sh' in their language. So none of the natives could have told anyone that they were "Ijaws". Fifty years after independence, the Izons are still trying to ensure that they are called by their true name.

Due to severe limitation of class and dormitory spaces in comparison to the population, admission to government secondary schools was extremely competitive. Of course, there were very good religious schools run by all the respective Christian denominations in southern Nigeria. The Catholics and Anglicans were most active, but there was significant activity by the Baptists and Methodists as well. There were also a number of private schools, but their resources were not comparable to those of the government schools.

Admission into the government secondary schools was through a Common Entrance Examination. Students taking the examination were asked to indicate some preferences if accepted, but it was largely determined by regions. Based upon the performance of the students, a number were invited to on-campus interviews and the available slots were filled from the group of those who had scored the highest, and a small waiting list was created. Some were lucky enough to get two admissions and had a chance to choose. Others who were admitted were unable to attend for personal or financial reasons, and then people were called up from the waiting list to fill any vacancies.

Even though primary school lasted through Standard Six, students were allowed to take the common Entrance Examination starting in Standard Five. Since I had done quite well in Standard Four, I was encouraged by my teachers to take the examination in Standard Five. Students were allowed to try many times, in standard five, six and even after leaving primary school.

I applied to take the examination in May or June, 1954. The nearest center was in Warri, about half a day's boat ride from Bomadi. We had to go there a day before, to be sure to arrive early at the designated site on the day of the examination. We were tested on English language, Arithmetic and General Knowledge. The General Knowledge portion tested our awareness of cultural and social topics such as political events and common acronyms, such as WAAC for West African Airways Corporation. Once again, being from an isolated area without regular access to newspapers and radios was a severe liability.

This experience has had an effect on my behavior as a parent. While my children were growing up, I made sure that there was a variety of reading material in the house. I subscribed to the two daily newspapers in the city, the Tennessean in the morning and the Nashville Banner in the afternoon. I also subscribed to the weekly

Time magazine and the monthly Readers Digest and National Geographic magazines. My children never suspected what demons I was chasing away in all these activities. In a twist of irony, while my daughter was attending a magnet high school in a predominantly black neighborhood, she was often described by her teachers and peers as being a privileged kid, especially having two parents with doctoral degrees and employed as university professors. So in one generation, we had gone from being disadvantaged to being advantaged. We pray continuously that this rise will continue for many generations to come.

Recently, while writing about these stories, with my memory refreshed, I sought out my wife in the kitchen and told her one of the stories again. It might have been the story of the Groote Beer, or the scare over the total eclipse of the sun, or the Princeton soccer letter. After I had told the whole story, she asked me if I knew how many times she had heard that story in forty years. Apparently one of the requirements of being a good wife is to listen to the same stories over and over; I think this should be included in our marriage vows.

I thought I held my ground on the Language and arithmetic portions of the test, but could not compete on the general knowledge part. The city kids had a distinct advantage and besides some of them were much more familiar with the tests through private tutoring. Accordingly, they had all the available spots. But I received another reprieve.

Even though the Izons were the most populous group in the Delta, we lived mostly in remote villages and were not represented in the admitted pool of forty eight students. The principal, an English man named Mr. C.C. Carter, decided to call up nine Izons from the waiting list to fill two vacant slots. I ended up being one of the two accepted and started at Ughelli in September 1954, forgoing the rest of my primary education. I do not know if they had any name for this special selection, as the term affirmation action was not known. Maybe, there was a British equivalent of that term or this was just something they did in the colonies which in many cases were built up with very diverse ethnic groups as in Nigeria or India.

We were admitted in September because the school year ran from September to August in line with the year in Britain. Soon people realized that we did not such wide weather changes from winter to fall to spring and summer as they had in Britain. So the school year was changed from a September start to a January start. This was made in 1957, so we had to spend an extra term in one form that year. My class stayed this extra term in Class Three.

Even though I was the beneficiary of this colonial form of affirmative action, as my friends have good-natured reminded me for over fifty years, they all knew that it was justified through my performance in the school. At the end of the first year, I was about fourth in a class of twenty-four. By the end of the second year, I was at the top of the class and remained near the top for the rest of our studies. In our final examination, I was again at the top and it helped to gain me admission to Princeton University as described in the last chapter.

Each entering class was made up of two sections Alpha and Beta, of twenty-four students each. The curriculum for the West African School Leaving Certificate was five years long. So our school had a population of about 240 students. Later, two years of Higher school certificate were added for a class of 24. We studied the equivalent of the first year of University courses in the two years.

In 1995, I spent the summer at the Oak Ridge national Laboratories as an HBCU Faculty visiting engineer. Dr. Omatete was a full time employee there, and I spent week days at his home and commuted to Nashville on weekends for the ten-week duration of the program. During this period, we came up with the idea of forming an alumni association of GCU graduates. We named it Government College Ughelli Old Boys' Association in the Americas, GCU-OBA-America. There were similar groups active in the UK and in several cities in Nigeria, especially Lagos and Warri. I served as the founding treasurer until 2003, and Omatete has served as our President from the beginning.

We have held reunions at Washington, DC in 2003, at Orlando in 2005 and at Dallas in 2007. At our gatherings, even allowing for the fact that we were middle aged men trying to relive our teenage years, our wives thought our behavior odd, specially the American wives. It is clear that attending the school had left indelible marks on us all. First, from the name of our group, one could tell that it was an all-boys school. Most of our peer institutions were also all-boys. In Lagos, there was a comparable school for girls, Queen's College, Yaba. In all other places, girls were severely underserved and it was left to the Christian denominations to try to fill in this wide gap in educational opportunities. Things have improved significantly in this regard since independence.

Our experiences paid equal attention to academics and character education. On a typical weekday, we woke up at a bell at 6 AM. We spent an hour cleaning our dormitory grounds and rooms. Then we dressed and went to class for two periods. We headed to our dining room for breakfast about 9 AM. After breakfast, we went back to classes until about 2 PM. This was followed by lunch. We then went to our dormitories for an hour of rest called siesta. Then we got out for two hours of either athletic activity, or general grounds-keeping in the areas outside our dormitories. After, we showered and dressed for dinner. After dinner, we had two hours of studying, about 7 to 9 PM and the junior boys were sent to bed, with lights out at about 9:30 PM. The seniors had an additional hour of studying and their lights out at about 10:30 PM. This routine was strictly enforced and coming late to any event would incur various levels of punishment, doing additional grounds-keeping work during the free periods on Saturdays.

There was also strict discipline and respect for those in higher classes. For example, those in class one had to obey instructions from those in class two and so on up the ladder. At the top of the hierarchy were student leaders called Prefects, who had jurisdiction not only in their respective houses, but also throughout the school. Our dormitories were called Houses and throughout my stay, there were five of these. The first was called School House, where I was assigned. The others were Warri House, Forcados House, Sapele House and Ashaka House. Several more were built after my time. These houses were named after medium cities and towns in the Delta.

We had serious internal competition between houses in track and field, soccer and cricket, with a house champion crowned in each sport every year. There were silver trophies for every sport and there was fierce competition to collect these trophies year after year. The winning house was inscribed on each trophy, so the history was displayed. We also had distinct colors for each house on our athletic shirts and jerseys. Yellow was the color for School House, red for Warri House, light blue for Forcados House, green for Sapele House and dark blue for Ashaka House. Because School House was the first, yellow was also the color for GCU in sports competition with other secondary schools. In the 1960s, we produced several athletics that represented Nigeria in Olympic and Commonwealth games.

Two faculty members were assigned to each house, called House Master and House Tutor. They selected members of the senior classes as house prefects. The principal selected the school prefects and they were given brass badges of office. One of the school prefects was designated as the head prefect at each house, called Head of House. One was also designated as the head prefect of the school, called Head of School. I was a school prefect in 1960 and Head of School House in 1961. Decades after graduation, we still jokingly treat each other as we did while at GCU, and it was always a source of amusement for our spouses. Because the Izons were small in number, I was protective of them and years later, they had stories of how I had saved them from punishment by those in intermediate classes.

The last time I visited GCU was in 1983. The family was driving from Lagos to Port Harcourt through Benin City, Warri and Ughelli, so we took a small detour off the

East-West Highway to see the school. My family, who had heard so much about it, was quite disappointed at its appearance and so was I. It was during a break and no students were on the campus. The lawns were overgrown, and the paint on School House was in very poor state. It was experiences like this that has motivated the Old Boys to try to bring it back to its old glory. We had learned that our school was modeled after such English icons as Eton and Harrow, and we expected it to stand the test of time for centuries. It will take a lot of work to achieve our dream.

The Old Boys are not the only ones devoted to the school. Mr. V.B.V. Powell who had been principal for over a decade, from 1945 to 1953, retired back to England after independence in 1960. However, he had willed that his ashes should be returned to GCU for burial and this was done in 1995 at the fiftieth anniversary of the founding of the school.

In 1958, oil was discovered in the Niger Delta and the wealth derived from crude oil exports has been good for all Nigeria, but the environment of the Niger Delta has paid an enormous price for this prosperity. Today, it is a troubled region, with no solution in sight. Let us hope for happier ending in the future.

GCU itself has lived up to the expectations of its founders. It has produced leaders of all kinds, from generals and admirals, to federal ministers and senators, and state governors and commissioners. There have been hundreds of university professors, doctors, lawyers and chief executives of private companies and government parastatals such as a petroleum refinery and a steel manufacturer.

8: SOME GCU IZON STUDENTS, 1959

CHAPTER EIGHT

Bomadi: 1953-1954, 1962

I had two brief stops in this town, two years as a primary school student, and six months as a secondary school teacher before going to the university. The status of the town has grown as Nigeria went through successive political subdivisions. Before Independence, it was a district government headquarters in the Western Region. Later, it became part of the Mid-West Region and then part of Bendel State and now part of Delta State. Its relative prominence is perhaps due to its location at the split of two channels of the River Niger as it flowed towards the Atlantic Ocean.

I have fond memories of those stops because each ended with me taking giant steps forward on my peculiar life journey. In September, 1954, I left to attend Government College, Ughelli. In June 1962, I left to start preparing for my journey to the United States and Princeton University.

The name Bomadi, or as the Izons pronounce it, "BOMOUNDI", means "looking at the sand bar or beach". This is in reference to half-mile long sandy beach created by the river at the split, stretching about a hundred yards to the left fork and much more on the right fork. Half of the town was built overlooking the beach, spreading about two miles along the right fork and about half a mile deep. In the upstream parts of Izonland, before the river flows had slowed down into the coastal swamps, the river bends and swerves between its banks, depositing sand bars first on one bank, and then on the other bank. The Izons refer to the banks of the river, not as left bank or right bank, but as the cliff side or the sand beach side. We call them "ASA" and "ETOKO". The river is deeper on the cliff side and the flow velocity is also higher on the cliff side. There is also more erosion on the cliff side. Since the flood sometimes covers the beach side for several months of the year, its land is more fertile and most farming plots are located above the sand beaches. Most Izon villages are located on the banks across from the sand bar. Bomadi is one of a few that are located on the side and beside the sand bar.

Facing south in the direction of the flow toward the ocean, the left fork flows through a number of villages with relative significance to the Izons. I have already mentioned the villages between Bomadi and Isampou: Anyamasa, Tuomo and Aleibri. After Isampou, there are Ekeremo, Torugbene, Ojobo, and Peretoru. Each village is best known for the prominent citizens it has spurned, according to Izon tradition and culture. The right fork also passes through a number of villages located on either left or right bank of the river at regular intervals. It eventually ends up, after more twists and splits in the mangrove trees and swamps of the delta, in Warri, Forcados or Burutu on the coast. Going up river were other Izon towns such as Patani, Odi and Kaiama, which are on the major East-West roads and link Izonland to the Urhobos and Isokos, and eventually to the Igbos in cities like Asaba, currently the headquarters of Delta State, and Onitsha, a large Igbo trading center.

After choosing to come to the NA school in Bomadi to complete the last three years of my primary education, I found that my relatives did not actually live in Bomadi, but in the adjacent villages. One relative from my father's side of the family lived in Kpakiama, just upstream from Bomadi and within view on the opposite bank of the river. The other group of relatives lived downstream in Anyamasa, about thirty minutes by paddle boat. I chose to stay with the relatives at Anyamasa, as I was closer to them.

When I took my wife to visit Isampou in 1983, she noticed that my relatives from my mother's side were much more enthusiastic in welcoming me and showing their pride in my accomplishments. They had taken care of me and paid my school fees while I was growing up. My relatives from my father's side were more subdued and on the sideline. In most Izon communities, and particularly those where polygamy is practiced, those related by a common mother were closer than relatives from a common father. We use the term for a relative, "BENA" loosely for brothers and sisters, uncles and aunts, and all levels of cousins. But when it really matters, we use the terms "KENI YIN BO ZI OTU" and "KENI DAU BO ZI OTU" to distinguish between the descendants of one's mother from the descendants of the father. As an early teen, when I should have been able to speak at family disputes over farming and fishing rights, which were largely inherited matrilineally, some of my aunts always cut me short, saying I was going to be living in the cities, and would not have to depend on those rights for my sustenance in life as they had to.

There were variations in our matrilineal tendencies, as I was very close to relatives through my mother's father. In fact, my uncle, James Ayama, my mother's father's only son, took particular interest in me, including following me to Ughelli for my campus interview because I was quite small at the time. He also paid for my expenses during my HSC years. He had a variety of careers, as a seaman, timber logger, and retail shop keeper. People thought he acted in an enlightened manner in his treatment of me. The last time I saw him was in 1966, in the port of Brooklyn on board a ship that he was working on; I was then attending Columbia University. He died before I returned to Nigeria in 1982. One of his grandchildren lives in New Jersey with his wife and children, two daughters and a son. I have attended the high school graduations of both young ladies; one is now a student in the Newark Campus of Rutgers University, and the other is a student on the New Brunswick campus. They were born in Lagos and never met this paternal great-grandfather, their father's mother's father. But he is the one I think of as I enjoy my own relationship with them.

As the present government units in Izonland are grappling with, the Izon villages are so dispersed that it was impossible to provide public amenities for each village. So schools, health clinics and such were located in some villages and those in adjourning villages were expected to travel there to be served. In 1953, there were a number of boat-pools of students commuting from Anyamasa to attend school in Bomadi. I joined one of these pools, leaving Anyamasa early enough to paddle to Bomadi to arrive at school before assembly at 8 AM. We commuters were given a ten-minute leeway before being sanctioned as late. It was a time of my life that I remember with great fondness.

The relatives that I lived with at Anyamasa are descendants of an older sister of my mother. I had gotten to know her well at various family gatherings, but she had died by the time I arrived in 1953. She was survived by two sons and three daughters who were all adults with children at the time. I felt very much at home among all of them, even though I stayed in the home of the younger son. The older son was then a seaman living mostly in Lagos when he was on shore leave from one of the ships he served on. I saw him in Lagos in 1962 before I left for the USA and I also visited with him in the port of Brooklyn during my Columbia days.

It seems that proportionately, the Izons were over represented among the Nigerian seamen in the British merchant fleet. Because of their comfort in the water environment, this was a natural occupation for them, whereas some of the members of inland ethnic groups could not swim and were deadly afraid of water, whether river or ocean. The Izons who served on merchant ships during World War II survived German submarine attacks in the Atlantic War, and were veterans entitled to certain benefits. My own father-in-law was one of them and had also served in the British army in Burma. He was issued a card, certifying his status as a veteran. He gave this card to his daughter during his final illness, urging her to collect pension benefits after his death. But due to loss of records after the war and the political upheavals in Nigeria, we have not been able to receive any benefits and are just keeping the card as a family souvenir.

My first stay at Bomadi ended happily when I was admitted to GCU. At GCU, I took and passed the West African School Certificate in 1959. I was then selected among a class of about twenty to continue for the Higher School Certificate. We took our HSC examinations in December 1961, and waited for the results to be returned from Cambridge University in the UK before we could apply for university admission in September. So there was a nine-month break between when we finished high school and when we could start attending university. It was common practice in this situation to work temporarily as entry-level civil servants or as junior high school teachers. I chose to teach in order to stay close to classrooms, and picked an offer from St. Brendan's Catholic School, Bomadi, over an offer from a private school in Warri. While I enjoyed my work with the mostly Izon student body and faculty, knowing that it could be the last time that I might serve my own people, it nearly cost me opportunity to go to the USA due to the late telegram, as I have stated in the Princeton chapter.

I have met some of the students I taught in those few months who are all grown up to be professionals and senior civil servants and politicians. They told me that what I taught them most was not the mathematics and Latin in the classroom, but as one of the role model motivating them to aspire to university education and studying abroad.

The last time I visited Bomadi was in 1983, soon after I started working full time at the University of Science and Technology, Port Harcourt. The registrar at the university,

Mr. Mieyebo, who haled from Bomadi, lost his father at that time. A full complement of the administration, faculty and staff went with him to perform his responsibilities as a prominent son. We arrived in the afternoon, danced throughout the night, and left the following afternoon. I took the opportunity to say hello to my relatives, and saw how the town had grown. It was a small haven of progress in Izonland.

9: VISIT WITH RELATIVES, PORT HARCOURT, 2005

CHAPTER NINE

Isampou: Birth To 1952

I was born in the village of Isampou, the fourth village down stream from Bomadi on the left bank of what is sometimes called the Bomadi-Isampou River. At the time I lived there, the river was about one hundred yards in the dry season, December to May, and swells to about one hundred and fifty yards during the floods in the rainy season. The river cycles were altered when the Kainji Hydroelectric Dam was built upstream to produce electricity for all of Nigeria in the 1970s. The river used to flow at a fast clip, especially in the flood stage. This was not only important for the fishing and farming activities, but also helped to keep the water at an acceptable degree of sanitation, as all the villages upstream used the river as sewage dump. It was the flow and the feeding of fishes on the raw sewage that maintained the barely acceptable quality of the river as a source of drinking water.

With the problems of water quality, and infestation by mosquitoes and other insects, this was a hazardous for humans, especially children. Infant mortality was high, even though reasonably accurate official figures were scarce. Almost every mother had lost a child in infanthood and probability of survival to adulthood was about seventy percent.

I was the last child of my mother, and the only child she had with my father. She had three other sons and she told me of a daughter who died, although I did not learn at what age. Her oldest son was already married when I was born, and in fact had a son about a week before I was born. I thus have a nephew of my own age. He has been living in Maryland for the last thirty years and has three children and five grandchildren. I have had a wonderful relationship with this set of grand nephews and nieces, and the great-grand nephews and nieces.

Being the last child provided some advantages for survival in the environment I grew up in. All mothers breastfed their babies, and while they were having babies in their natural cycles, they had to be weaned in a little over a year. But as the last child, one could breastfeed until eighteen months or more. Apparently, I must have broken a record for the duration of breastfeeding. Growing up, I was teased extensively about how long I continued to feed even after the nutritional value must have disappeared. I might have imagined it from the teasing, but I almost could remember being breastfed, which must have been at least two years or more. By a twist of faith, my wife was also the last child of her mother, but being raised in Lagos, she did not have the same experience that I had.

One of the other jokes was that when my mother had occasion to baby sit her first grandson, she could also be a wet nurse for him. This might have been a quite common situation since in those days without any method of birth control, girls got married in their teens and had babies until their early forties. I often teased him that he was much taller than me because he had two sources of milk as a baby, his mother and my mother/his grandmother. But of course genetics might have played a bigger role in selecting his stature. His mother was quite tall, and he also had a sister who was tall.

It was such that I was quite sickly as a child. I had regular bouts of malaria, yellow fever and jaundice. I also had a touch of epileptic seizures and fainting spells. Most of the treatment available was by use of certain roots, barks and leaves. If my uncle was around, then I could get a few doses of quinine and aspirin. When I started school and began to receive attention for my grades, my mother's fear that I would be harmed by witchcraft from jealous neighbors and other evil spirits, was heightened. I was unwillingly pulled to herbalists who administered several rounds of antidotes for my protection, some involving painful cuts throughout my body and rubbing medicinal powders on them. Some of these cuts are still visible on my legs, arms, chest and head.

There was no school in Isampou before 1948. The nearest Native Administration school was in Aleibri, a few miles upstream. A few enlightened parents had sent their sons to attend there. With the hazards of commuting, it was not considered safe for girls, so only boys attended. How ever, a small Anglican church had been established at Isampou and it met for services at a small hall belonging to one of the members. What the church needed were people who could read the gospels and the prayers from the Book of Common Prayer. There were both English and Izon language versions of these books. The Izon version was translated in the Kolokuma dialect, which was spoken by Izons from Patani to Odi and Kaiama up the river from Bomadi. There was also a version in the Nembe dialect, which was used by those in Brass and other areas to Otuan and Amasioama, as I learnt later from my wife and mother-in law who are from that part of Izonland. It was ironic that the leaders of the CMS church at Isampou could not read or write, but they were determined to teach their children to read and write. But the NA school at Aleibri was secular, and did not teach enough of the Anglican tradition to meet the requirements of the church lesders. So they were the main force behind establishment of a CMS school in Isampou.

The first attempt was made in 1947 when a teacher was brought from another town to operate a school. The school was located in the same hall that was used as a church on Sundays. The students were divided into approximate class levels indifferent corners of the room and the teacher circulated among the groups teaching different subjects and assigning work before moving to another group. I was just about the right age to attend school and one of my relatives took me down and enrolled me in the beginning infant class. But I did not want to go to school, making an argument that has been echoed to me by my older relatives for over fifty years.

My reason for not wanting to stay in school was that I did not wish to relocate to another town or city and leave my mother behind. Somehow, I had observed that those who got an education even just up to Primary Six were no longer fit for the village life nor had any desire to live it. They either went for training to become teachers or they went to the cities such as Warri or as far as Lagos to work as clerks. Since we had not had a school in Isampou, the teachers also went elsewhere to teach in schools in other villages, far or near. I just did not want to be part of them. So after a day or two, I left and stopped attending. After several attempts at persuading me, my relative gave up.

When I went to visit Isampou in 1982, I heard the rest of the story. After I left for Lagos in 1962, I did not see my mother again. Some of my relatives came to the airport to see me off to the USA and later reported to my mother how I had gone off in an airplane. They told me that when ever an airplane flew over our village, my mother would wave at it and plead for it to go and get me back to her again. She died in her sixties while I was still a graduate student at Columbia. In my adult life ever since, when I got close to any elderly lady, my wife would tease me that I was just looking for a surrogate mother because I had not said good bye satisfactorily to my mother. Of course, when I left her in 1962, I expected to be away for only three years for my bachelor's degree. Then I would return to Nigeria, and live a middle class life as a senior civil servant. As it turned out, I did not get back to my village until twenty years later, and that was a three-day visit. If my mother had lived a little longer, I certainly would have made it back a decade earlier. I hope and pray that by writing it down, I have chased away for good, not only this one , but all the other demons of my life, and that I would live out the rest of my days with peace in my mind, body and soul.

I do not remember how long our school lasted in 1947.

The Anglican teacher soon found things difficult. He might have had trouble getting support from the Church Missionary Society, and being at a remote post, his salary was not being received regularly and the local sponsors could not pay him. So after four or five months, he quit and left town.

The members of the church were determined to try again. They built a new church at the end of the village closer to my home, with a separate residence for a teacher. Then they sent another teacher in 1950. My uncle Ayama sent my cousin and playmate, Anyama to enroll in the school. Seeing him in his school attire, and missing my constant companion, I decided on my own to go to school this time around. Whether I might have learnt something in 1947, I completed my kindergarten and first grade standards in that one year. Thereafter, I went one grade a year, Standard 2 in 1951, and Standard 3 in 1952.

At the end of the school year in 1951, I was part of the highest grade at the school. Our teacher wanted to introduce to us the option of transferring to the nearest Anglican school to complete the final grades of primary education. Unfortunately, this was in Patani, which was a day's journey in paddle boat in those days. He arranged with some of his colleagues at Patani for us to take the same end of year examinations. About ten of us made the trip with our teacher to Patani and took the tests in English, Arithmetic, Religious Knowledge and General Knowledge. Our class was about ten and their class was about forty or fifty. When the results were announced, our teacher was so proud that we had placed in the top five in most of the subjects. However, his hopes were not fulfilled. At the end of the following year, no one opted to continue with the Anglican education. Several of us went to the NA school at Bomadi, some went to the NA school at Aleibri and others just dropped out of school at the end of the third grade.

The hopes of our church leaders were soon realized. Starting as early as standard one, several of us were able to read the gospels and prayers in the Izon translation. I participated in our church activities diligently until I left for Bomadi in 1952. that is why i an somewhat fanatical participating in church activities, sering several terms as senior and junior warden, as well as a Stephen minister.

When I visited in 1982, they had recently completed another building because the former one had been destroyed by erosion. They proudly gave me a tour. Now the primary school had its own building at the other end of the village. It had all the primary grades, and there was a secondary school adjacent to it. So there was progress. In fact, I had played a minor role in establishing the high school. In 1962, before going to Lagos to secure my travel documents, the village leaders came to me and told me about the plan to propose the establishment of the school. The request for proposals had come from the Local Government headquarters in Bomadi as part of development planning after independence. Using my simple high school geometry set such as compass and protractor, I made scale drawings of floor plans, front and side elevations of classroom buildings, bathrooms and residential quarters for the teachers. I also made estimates for enrollment and other factors to support our application. They were pleased with my effort and subsequently submitted their proposal. The authorities had some questions and criticisms of the proposal, which apparently came as a surprise to the village leaders. They had so much confidence in me that they could not imagine me making mistakes or being criticized. One of the issues that was raised was that there was not enough bathroom space for the estimated student population. Not being an architect or civil engineer, I was not surprised at such oversight. I was told of all this consternation by my relatives who came to Lagos to see me off to the US. I was happy to see that they ended up with the high school they had wished for.

By the time I had spent two years at Government College, Ughelli, I began to view the beliefs and actions of the village as an outsider. For example, one of the final activities of the funeral of person above a certain age was a divination and conversation with the soul of the dead person. A short ladder ["obobo"] was constructed and held on the shoulders of four persons, with a leader on the right front corner. Certain questions were asked of the dead person and the person supposedly responded by turning right or left. The last crucial question was whether the person was a witch or not. If the answer was "Yes", then the celebration was cut off and the person was given a dishonorable burial. If the response was "No", then there was more celebration and the person was eventually accorded an honorable burial. I was told that the leader mostly determined which way to turn, and that he did so in a trance and could not remember afterwards which way he had turned. I was skeptical and wondered whether the leader was simply expressing the perceived prejudice of the community or simply responding to the standing and reputation of the survivors.

Years later, in the spring semester of my sophomore year at Princeton University, I took an introductory course in anthropology as part of the humanities and social science requirements for my engineering degree. The instructor, Professor Crabb, soon learned of my place of origin. Later, he told me that a certain colleague of his at Brown University, had done field work in cultural anthropology at an Izon village, and had studied the funeral practices of Izons, including this "OBOBO" practice. He then put me in contact with his colleague and I had several written and telephone conversations with him. That was in 1963. Years later, in 1989, my wife was writing a doctoral thesis on nutritional practices of women at an Izon village and her literature search included extensive reference to the work of the professor from Brown. It is truly a small world.

After almost fifty years of living in the United States and learning to understand the minds and souls of my fellow citizens, I feel like I have been engaged in practicing reverse anthropology. I have been fascinated by their beliefs and assumptions about life here and after, good and evil, right and wrong, similar to what anthropologists have studied about the Izons. This is partially the purpose for the next and last chapter of this book. Of course, anthropologists usually spend six to eighteen months of living with a primitive culture before presenting their analysis of that culture. In my case, being an amateur, it has taken half a century for me to venture publication of my observations about a civilized culture.

After decades of anthropologists from the western world questioning and analyzing the beliefs of the Izons, it is fair to apply the same analysis to their beliefs as well. Of course, anthropologists have a reputation of respecting the beliefs and the idols that symbolize those beliefs. In contrast for example, the Spaniards who came to colonize the lands of the Aztecs and Incas had the intention that said to the Native-Americans as follows: My idols are more powerful than your idols, so I will take away your idols and give you my crucifixes, madonnas and saints; and when I get back to Spain, I will melt down and extract all the gold and silver from your idols and live a life of wealth for the rest of my days.

10: THREE DR. AWIPIS, 2009

CHAPTER TEN

Assessment

As my title indicates, I want this to be, in part, an assessment of my life. I wish to seek answers to questions such as these:

What was the purpose for my life?

How much of that purpose have I fulfilled?

What more can I do in the remaining days of my life to fulfill more of my purpose for existence?

Of course, I am fully aware that these and related questions have been asked by mankind for many thousands of years, in many continents, cultures and religious traditions. The answers have also varied in time and place. Some answers are based on our current state of scientific knowledge, and once we exceed the limits of knowledge, we rely on religious beliefs for answers. My life has provided me with a unique perspective on the boundary between knowledge and belief. I have been painfully aware of the possibility of belief based on ignorance rather than the limit of knowledge. In my life, I have found plenty of reason to fear the power of ignorance, the third power in the Gnostic Gospel of Mary and to embrace the joy of knowledge. Let me give a few examples of what I mean.

When I was growing up, the Izons believed in witches who flew to meeting places in the middle of the night where they would dance and perform evil rituals until near daybreak. One of the prices for admission into this wicked club was alleged to be the sacrifice of a close family member, such as a grandchild or nephew or niece. The more precious the sacrifice, the higher the esteem accorded by the covey of witches, although it was not clear what were the benefits of membership: they were not more prosperous than others and there was no promise of immortality as in the legend of Dracula. This was the best explanation the society provided for the high rate of infant and child mortality. A lot of energy and resources were devoted to identifying the witches and wizards in the village so that they could be avoided and ostracized. Unfortunately, during periods of social chaos, these suspects were murdered because they were blamed for every misfortune that befalls the clan. During the Biafran civil war in Nigeria from 1967 to 1970, many innocent elderly women were murdered for this reason. As an adult, I now know that the high infant and child mortality rate was due to poor hygiene, contaminated drinking water, malaria carrying mosquitoes and other parasites, compounded by inadequate medical care. Also, many of the queer behavior patterns that were used to identify witches, such as sleeplessness and irritability were simply symptoms of post menopausal depression. I vividly remember one special occasion, around 1953, when a lady who claimed to have the ability to identify witches was brought to our village. After paying her a lot of money, every adult was paraded before her and she fingered a good number of men and women for being members. This was nearly three hundred years after the Salem witch trials (1692) and more than one hundred years after the final suppression of the Spanish Inquisition (1834).

Another case wherein great evil was committed for a belief based on ignorance was Aztec human sacrifice in Mexico which the Spaniards witnessed in 1510. The Aztecs believed that some of their gods and even the sun required the energy from blood in a beating heart to maintain their functions and blessings on them. For example, without an adequate supply of sacrificial blood, the sun would stop its motion and prolonged darkness would ensue, disrupting agricultural production and causing famine. As every school child knows, from the works of Nicolas Copernicus (1543), Galileo Galilei (1632) and Isaac Newton (1687), the motions of the sun and its planets, including the earth are governed by laws of gravitation and did not require blood sacrifices to maintain their orbits. Both Copernicus and Galileo were soundly persecuted for their ideas, the prevailing doctrine of the Roman Catholic Church at the time was that the earth was stationary and flat, with the sun, moon and other heavenly bodies revolving around the earth; this particularly befitted the home of human beings who had been created in the image of God and made masters of all living things on earth and perhaps of the universe. The sun is occasionally darkened by eclipses and by heavy clouds of volcanic ash which were usually causes for major panic. It has also been suggested, in a History Channel program entitled " The Exodus Decoded" that the darkness over ancient Egypt before the exodus of the Hebrews was caused by volcanic ash.

Many other societies and cultures experienced these natural phenomena, but did not formulate bloody religious beliefs and practices in response. I was an eyewitness to mass panic in our village during a particularly deep and prolonged solar eclipse around 1949 and later, in 1970, I witnessed the joyful anticipation and viewing of another solar eclipse in New York City. The contrast in the reactions to similar natural events in the two locations has left an indelible mark in my mind ever since. Unexplained natural phenomena, such as floods, earthquakes, volcanic eruptions have been the sources of many religious practices, myths and legends. Again, we are all familiar with the story of Noah's ark, or the worshiping of gods believed to reside inside the volcanoes of the Hawaiian islands

As engineers, we have a common admonition not to re-invent the wheel, and for electrical engineers, the transistor. So let me discuss contemporary views of why human beings were created or how they came to be and the purpose of their existence. I will

start with the Catechism of the Catholic Church, the Catechism of the Church of England in which I was baptized and confirmed, and finally the very popular book by Rick Warren, "The Purpose Driven Life" (2002). Since I was baptized into the Anglican Church and I am currently a member of the Episcopal Church U.S.A. which as of this writing in October, 2006 is a member of the world-wide Anglican Communion, how did I get involved with the Catechism of the Catholic Church? Well, for two years, I attended a secular local government operated primary school, 1953 to 1954. Moral Education was part of the curriculum, and the teacher who taught this part happened to have been a very devout Catholic, and to him, moral or character education was equivalent to religious education and religion meant the Catholic Church. There was no companion to the American Civil Liberties Union to protest his action. So I remember a lesson similar to the sequence of questions and answers below, from the New Saint Joseph Catechism (1964):

1. Who made us?
    God made us.

2. Who is God?
    God is the Supreme Being who made all things.

3. Why did God make us?
    God made us to show forth His goodness and to share with us His everlasting happiness in heaven.

4. What must we do to gain the happiness of heaven?
    To gain the happiness of heaven we must know, love, and serve God in this world.

The above sequence is a simplified form, intended for instruction of young

minds. An adult version of the Catechism (1994), Part One, Section 356,

Man is described as follows:

" Of all visible creatures only man is able to know and

love his creator. He is the only creature on earth that God has willed for its own sake, and he alone is called

to share, by knowledge and love, in God's own life. It was for this end that he was created, and this is the fundamental reason for his dignity."

I have pondered this lesson for over fifty years. God made us to eventually share heaven with God, but to gain heaven, we must know, love and serve God in this world. There are two issues that I need to resolve; there were already angels sharing heaven with God before man was created, and inevitably, there will be a certain proportion of men and women who did not do enough of knowing, loving and serving God in this world, and so would not fulfill their purpose of sharing heaven with God. That would be inefficient, and besides, if there was more room in heaven, God might have created more angels who are assured of being good enough for heaven, instead of trying to turn human beings into angels. I believe I have seen and learnt about the best and the worst of the human species in all history, and even at our best, we are not angels, although some have been saints. If billions of human beings have been created since the beginning of time in order to filter out a few million angels at the end of time, whether the ratio is one angel out of thousands or tens of thousands, it smacks of survival of the fittest, and evolution.

The Catechism of the Episcopal Church USA, contained in the 1979 Book of Common Prayer, has a number of questions and answers on Human Nature without specifically stated why we were created or what our purpose in life could be:

Q.	What are we by nature?

Q.	We are part of God's creation, made in the image of God.

Q.	What does it mean to be created in the image of God?

A.	It means that we are free to make choices; to love, to create, to reason, and to live in harmony with creation and with God.

Q.	Why then do we live apart from God and out of harmony with creation?

A.	From the beginning, human beings have misused their freedom and made wrong choices.

Q.	Why do we not use our freedom as we should?

Q.	Because we rebel against God, and we put ourselves in the place of God.

Q.	What help is there for us?

Q.	Our help is in God.

Q.	How did God first help us?

Q.	God first helped us by revealing himself and his will, through nature and history, through many seers and saints, and especially through the prophets of Israel.

One cannot help but make comparisons between the catechisms of the Catholic and Episcopal Churches as related to man's place and purpose in creation. The Episcopal Church is more comfortable with the place of man as a part of creation without subtracting from his dignity, and that man should incorporate reason in his beliefs. This allows us to revise our beliefs as more certain scientific knowledge becomes available. As it became certain that the earth was not the center of the solar system, not to talk of the universe, we adjusted to it. If in the future, we come into contact with other beings almost as intelligent as , or more intelligent than us, somewhere in the universe, we will adjust our beliefs to the known facts again. We hope that if they get to our planet first, they will not plant some flag and claim us for their king , queen, emperor, or president, whatever their ruler might be. If we get to their planet or place of abode first, we hope not to claim them and their land for our president. Also, if they have found answers to the question of the reason and purpose for their creation and existence, we hope they will be glad to share their answers with us, and we will be glad to share our answers with them. We hope they will not impose their answers on us, and that we will not impose our answers on them. Of course, if we ever receive visitors from a more advanced group of beings, most people would wish to get more practical benefits from them other than simply sharing answers on the meaning and purpose of life; if their medical technology is really advanced and they understood our physiology, they might help us to find cures for some of our most deadly diseases such as various cancers and heart disease, thereby enabling us to double or triple our life spans.

While the answers to the meaning and purpose of life questions provided by the catechisms of the Catholic and Anglican churches have been available for hundreds of years, a stream of recent interpretations of these answers continue to emanate from Christian sources.

Several of these that I have examined are the following. First is the book " Power For Living " (1983) by Jamie Buckingham, commissioned by the Arthur S. DeMoss Foundation. The main theme of this book is that success in this life is meaningful only if it is coupled with a personal relationship with God through belief in Jesus Christ. This is primarily based on Isaiah 40:31 : " But those who wait on the Lord will find new strength. They will fly high on wings like eagles. They will run and not grow weary. They will walk and not faint. " Eleven well known individuals from various fields of human endeavor who have found this kind of lasting real success also gave personal testimony to the validity of the main theme of the book.

Another modern interpretation is contained in the book " The Purpose Driven Life " (2002) by Rick Warren. In this book, the author helps the reader to discover the meaning and purpose of life by recognizing that man was made by God and for God; he identifies five purposes for human life:

Purpose #1: You were planned for God's Pleasure;

Purpose #2: You were formed for God's Family;

Purpose #3: You were created to become like Christ;

Purpose #4: You were shaped for serving God;

Purpose #5: You were made for a mission.

The reward for accomplishing these purposes during our temporary existence on earth is to spend eternity with God in heaven; as stated by Reverend Warren:

" Your time on earth is not the complete story of your life. You must wait until heaven for the rest of the chapters." This agrees with the Catholic catechism that God created human beings so that a selected proportion could become angels and live with God in heaven.

Still another modern interpretation of the reason for human existence is provided by The Meaning of Life Project which was started by personal performance and productivity coach Joe Mathews in 2001.Confining itself to life on earth, it seeks to define success by who has the most satisfying relationships, the greatest balance between life and work, and whose life and career made the most difference in the lives of others.

These four interpretations of the reason for the creation of human beings and therefore the purpose for our life on earth are based on the creation stories in the book of Genesis in the Hebrew Bible which is mostly identical with the Old Testament of the Christian Bible. Since the founders of the religion of Islam also claim to be descendants of Abraham of the Hebrew/Old Testament bible, I guess that they also subscribe to the creation stories in Genesis, although I am not personally very knowledgeable about their religion. My only reason for this statement is to surmise that with the combined population of believers in Judaism, Christianity and Islam, about one third of present human race, over two billion persons believe this set of creation stories. Again these are religious stories and not scientific facts, so it may not be useful to compare them to other stories currently being believed by the other two thirds of the human race, mostly in Asia. But there are lessons to be learned by comparing our current beliefs to those of other times and places, such as Horus of Ancient Egypt,

Zeus of Ancient Greece, and Pele of native Hawaii. The last is quite interesting because it is a female creator God similar to the Izon TAMARAU or WOYINGI [She who creates or Our Mother]. The original Hawaiians observed the lava flowing into the sea, cooling and enlarging their island world and surmised that this was the way the whole world was created. Since the lava flow was also similar to menstrual flow, they figured that the crater of the volcano was the vagina of the Creator and therefore prohibited men from looking down into the crater. The belief in this female creator also was the justification of having queens and princesses as their traditional rulers and priests, and explains the ritual of throwing young males into the crater. At the same time, I respect any society that was able to create a God in their own image. Too often, people and cultures co-opted the God created by others (Yahweh, Allah) or were forced to accept other people's God at the point of a sword or the barrel of a gun. Which of our most cherished beliefs will be labeled as mythology and superstition a thousand years from now?

In Genesis 1:1, we read that " In the beginning, God created the heaven and the earth."

So far, no reason or purpose was given for God embarking on the creation enterprise.

But in Genesis 1: 3-4, we read that "And God said, Let there be light: and there was light. And God saw the light, that it was good." The last phrase was repeated after every stage of creation and supports the interpretation that God was pleased with His creation after the fact, even though it was not stated that pleasure was the motivation for the act of creation.

Also, the implication that light was created after the earth is astronomically puzzling, since all the light we see on the earth comes from the sun, directly on half of the earth during the day, and indirectly by reflection off the moon on the other half at night, with small contributions from other stars and reflections from other planets of the solar system. Also, since the earth is a planet of the sun, it clearly could not exist before the sun was created.

The creation of the rest of the biological world then follows in reasonable order: plant life on the third stage, fishes and birds on the fifth stage and animal life on the sixth stage. At this stage, we read in Genesis 1: 27-28 " ..God created man in his own image, in the image of God created he him; male and female created he them. And God blessed them, and God said unto them, Be fruitful and multiply, and replenish the earth, and subdue it: and have dominion over the fish of the sea, and over the fowl of the air, and over every living thing that moveth upon the earth" Here, human beings have been given two directives: to multiply and to have dominion over the earth. These are the two purposes for human existence.

What are our rewards for accomplishing these purposes? The first purpose provides what constitutes immortality while the second provides for our sustenance as we pursue the first. The first provides a design for immortality because every offspring carries half of Each parent's genetic material. In a perfect execution of this process, let the parent have two offspring, and let each offspring have two children who now have one quarter of each grandparent's genes, and so on. As this process continues, each generation has a smaller fraction of the ancestor's genes but there are more members in each generation and the product of the fraction and the number of members of each generation always equals one. In mathematical illustration:

First generation: 1 Member

2nd generation: ½ Genetic material times 2 members = 1

3rd generation: 1/4 genetic material times 4 members = 1

4th generation: 1/8 genetic material times 8 members = 1

5th generation: 1/16 genetic material times 16 members = 1

This sequence continues to infinity, and as many of us learned from high school

Algebra II, the infinite geometric series with initial value ½ and common

ratio ½ sums to 1:

That is, $\frac{1}{2} + \frac{1}{4} + \frac{1}{8} + \frac{1}{16} + \frac{1}{32} + \frac{1}{64} + \ldots = 1$.

Mankind has sought immortality for all of its existence, but only genetic immortality is biologically provided for at our current stage of knowledge. Other forms of immortality that we seek start us on a slippery slope:

BELIEF
|
|
SPECULATION
|
|
PROPHESY
|
|
MYTHOLOGY
|
|
SUPERSTITION.

There is a lesson somewhere around here for those who engage in culture wars with the premise that "What I believe is Truth and what you believe is Superstition". Historically, this has resulted in cultural colonialism, which went along with economic colonialism and political colonialism. Until we know, it seems reasonable to keep a bit of open mind on alternative cosmologies.

Long before mankind learned of genes and DNA, we have gone to great lengths in our search for immortality, and independently we have sought to reproduce as all other living things, plants, fishes, birds, insects, and of course, the animal world; we now know that these two primal imperatives and desires are linked. When Marlowe's Dr. Faustus asked Helen to make him immortal with a kiss, he knew or should have been advised that he would have had to go much further to get to the first base in the sequence of immortality. The late Princess Diana of Great Britain was said to have been depressed that, after her two sons were described as a heir and a spare, she felt like a choice cow put out to be bred by a stud bull and all the adulation that her subjects showered on her did not quite succeed in cheering her up. Maybe the thought she has reached first base in the quest for immortality might have done the trick. Knowing that our individual existence started as a speck of DNA, perhaps it is appropriate that at the end we scatter as specks of DNA. We human beings have a sense that the way we end should match the way we began, hence the phrase " dust to dust" is included in the Christian burial rite. As was reported in the New York Times on November 9, 2006, there is some possibility that even the Neanderthals, who became extinct about 30,000 years ago, still have portions of their DNA in the human gene pool through some chance interbreeding with members of Homo Sapiens in the short period that they co-existed on earth.

Of course, achieving immortality as specks of DNA is not much fun and no religion that I am aware of has offered this form of immortality as an attractive article of faith. On the other hand, singing and dancing on needles for hundreds and thousands of years could be a challenge as well after a while, especially with no seventy virgins to play with. As the Count Dracula movies have tried to teach us, immortality is not all it might have been cooked up to be. You may wish to live ever after, but there is no guarantee that you will do so happily.

Let us return to the second directive of Genesis 1: 28 to subdue the earth, replenish it and have dominion over all living things on land, sea and air. Since we humans are not the biggest, the strongest or the fastest living things on earth, the only path to fulfillment of this directive has been our superior knowledge of the earth and all other living things. We have sometimes and in some cases gone beyond subduing to excessive exploitation, but overall, the search for knowledge and its propagation has been the noblest of human endeavors. I am glad to have been able to participate In the frontlines of this endeavor as an engineer and professor. Of course, as for a soldier in the frontline trenches of war, there are hundreds of supporting lines manufacturing and transporting the arms, ammunition and food necessary for the frontline soldier to accomplish his tasks and objectives. So it is for those in the frontline of the battle for creation, acquisition and propagation of knowledge. I will acknowledge the scores of teachers and professors who prepared me for the role of frontline soldier in the battle for knowledge, and have allowed me to fulfill one of the roles that I was created for.

I have balanced knowledge and belief, and I have avoided speculation, prophesy, mythology and superstition. We humans are very smart animals, but there is still a lot that we do not yet know about origin and purpose. It is advisable that we keep our minds open for future discoveries in the biological and astronomical sciences that can answer more of the eternal questions relating to our origin and purpose on earth. For me, the two directives from Genesis, to multiply and dominate the earth, which are so ingrained in our nature, are the surest purposes for our lives, even with no certainty as to our origin. I have been privileged to participate in both endeavors by becoming a parent, and by acquiring and contributing to knowledge, and transmitting it to the next generation. It has been a life well spent.

Finally, we know that everything has a beginning and an end and so we have birth and death, growth and decay. When I face death, my body will have carried me as far as it could and in its weakened state, I probably will not miss it much. But I will miss my mind which has carried me much further than I could ever have imagined. I hope I am not flattering my self too much to think that my family and friends will also miss me. I want to ask them to do two things for me and for themselves. First, I want my friends to help me to express my gratitude the Supernatural Being or Natural Force that we call the Creator of the universe, Whom I will probably never fully know, by singing this hymn at my funeral service.

It is hymn number 60 from Lift Every Voice and Sing II: "How Great Thou Art".

The first verse and the chorus are as follows:

"O Lord my God, when I in awesome wonder,
Consider all the worlds thy hands have made,
I see the stars, I hear the rolling thunder,
Thy pow'r throughout the universe displayed."

Chorus

"Then sings my soul, my Savior, God, to Thee;
How great Thou art, how great Thou art!
Then sings my soul, my Savior God, to Thee:
How great Thou art, how great Thou art! "

My second request is to sing a second hymn to comfort my grieving family and friends.
It is also from LEV II, number 147: Come ye Disconsolate.
Its first verse is as follows:

Mebenin Awipi

"Come, ye disconsolate, where'er ye languish,
Come to the mercy-seat, fervently kneel:
Here bring your wounded hearts, here tell your anguish;
Earth has no sorrow that heav'n cannot heal."